THE WELLAND CANALS
A COMPREHENSIVE GUIDE

JOHN N. JACKSON
FRED A. ADDIS

Prepared for the Welland Canals Foundation, Box 745, St. Catharines, Ontario, L2R 6Y3.

Printed by Lincoln Graphics, St. Catharines, Ontario.
Layout by Free Vision Communications, Ltd., St. Catharines, Ontario.

TABLE OF CONTENTS

cont'd. . . .

III. Ships and Trade on the Canal

IV. Canal Data and Information

Introduction

The outstanding feat of the Welland Canal is unexcelled anywhere else in the world. In no other country are large ocean-going vessels taken over a slope as abrupt and steep as the Niagara Escarpment. Nor are they to be found at such altitudes above sea level. Lake Ontario to the north has an average level of about 75 m (246 feet), and Lake Erie to the south an average level of about 174 m (572 feet).

The modern Canal covers this height difference of about 100 m (326 feet) by seven lift locks and one guard lock over a distance of some 43.44 km (27 miles), and is therefore the most difficult and the most spectacular section of the St. Lawrence Seaway. First achieved in 1829, the Welland Canal has remained in continuous operation (though on different routes and different alignments) since that date. It is the fourth in a continuous and notable series of significant waterways to connect the Upper and the Lower Lakes.

As an important part of the national heritage, Canadian canals lie mainly in the east of the country. All are now operated by the Federal Government, though the Welland Canal was initiated and operated by the private Welland

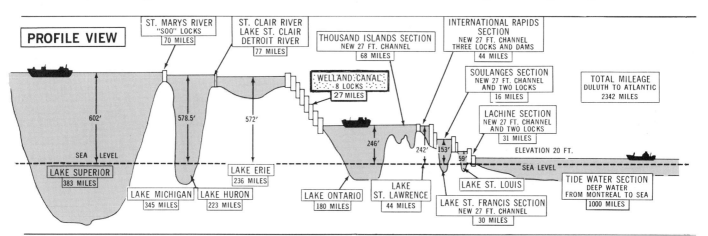

St. Lawrence Seaway Authority

Vessels using the Welland Canal, part of the St. Lawrence Seaway, overcome a height difference of 100 m (326 feet) between Lake Erie and Lake Ontario.

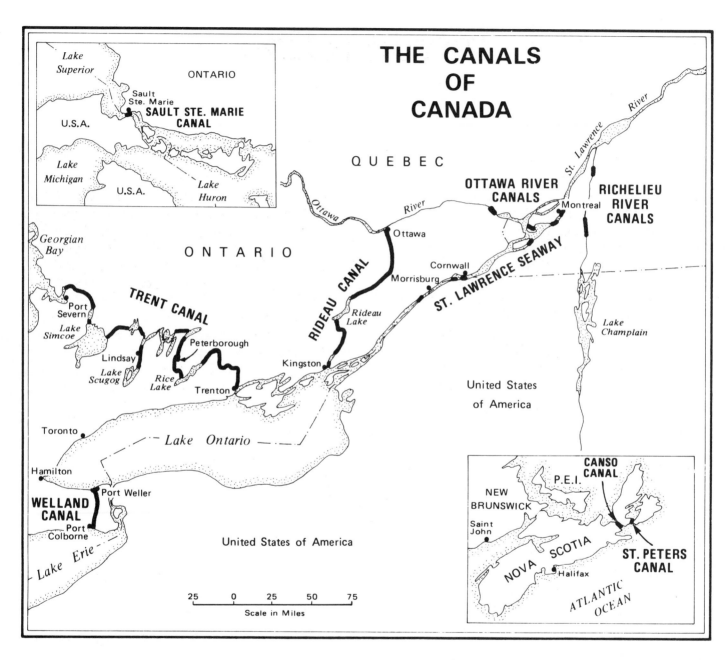

THE CANALS OF CANADA

Lake Superior
ONTARIO
Sault Ste. Marie
SAULT STE. MARIE CANAL
U.S.A.
Lake Michigan
U.S.A.
Lake Huron

QUEBEC

OTTAWA RIVER CANALS
Montreal
RICHELIEU RIVER CANALS

St. Lawrence River

Georgian Bay

ONTARIO

Ottawa

RIDEAU CANAL

Cornwall
Morrisburg

ST. LAWRENCE SEAWAY

Port Severn

TRENT CANAL

Lake Simcoe

Lindsay

Peterborough

Rideau Lake

Lake Scugog

Rice Lake

Trenton

Kingston

United States of America

Lake Champlain

Toronto

Lake Ontario

Hamilton

Port Weller

WELLAND CANAL

Port Colborne

Lake Erie

United States of America

25 0 25 50 75
Scale in Miles

CANSO CANAL
P.E.I.
NEW BRUNSWICK
Saint John
NOVA SCOTIA
Halifax
ST. PETERS CANAL
ATLANTIC OCEAN

Department of Geography, Brock University

Apart from a lock on the Red River, Canadian Canals are concentrated in Eastern Canada.

Canal Company in its early years. The most important representative of these canals in terms of route, scale, complexity and historic importance is undoubtedly the St. Lawrence Seaway system of navigation. It was, however, the prior achievement of the Welland Canal which allowed the Seaway to penetrate to the inland heart of the North American continent. The Welland Canal has played a vital role in the growth of important United States and Canadian interests around the Great Lakes, and is a key achievement of the North American economy.

John N Jackson

The St. Lawrence Seaway penetrates to the inland heart of the North American continent. Even so, this ship's name is rather optimistic.

3

I
Features and Characteristics
of the Welland Canal

1.1 The Need for a Canal

Why does the Welland Canal exist? Why was it necessary? The answer to these critical questions begins at the Niagara River, the natural outlet from Lake Erie to Lake Ontario. No ship can follow this foaming route across the Niagara Escarpment. The Rapids south of the Falls, the American and the Horseshoe Falls, and the Niagara Gorge with its Whirlpool, together present an impassable barrier to navigation. Some form of man-made achievement was imperative if Lake Erie and Lake Ontaro were to be interconnected for travel and the movement of goods, or if a direct route from the St. Lawrence to the Upper Great Lakes was to be achieved.

At first, an overland portage provided the answer. Goods were unloaded at Fort Niagara or at a landing where Lewiston, N.Y., is now located, then transported overland past the Falls, then trans-shipped back to water conveyances, and hauled up the Niagara River to Lake Erie for conveyance on the Lake. The task was arduous, time consuming, costly and dangerous. With American Independence in 1783 and the establishment of British Upper Canada, this portage

Hugh J Gayler

The Niagara River drops abruptly at the Horseshoe Falls. First a portage, then the Welland Canal, bypassed this tempestuous section of the Niagara River.

was transferred to the Canadian Bank, an historic route that can now be traced as the Portage Road through Niagara Falls.

The Niagara Portage remained the route for transportation between Lake Erie and Lake Ontario until 1829, when the First Welland Canal opened as a major constructional achievement

4

WILLIAM H. MERRITT 1793-1862

Born in Bedford, New York, Merritt came to Upper Canada with his family in 1796 where his father, a Loyalist, acquired land near here on Twelve Mile Creek. During the War of 1812, Merritt served with the 2nd Lincoln Militia. Returning here after the conflict he became a successful merchant and mill-owner. Primarily responsible for the construction of the first Welland Canal 1824-29, he represented Haldimand in Upper Canada's legislature 1832-41 and Lincoln in the Legislative Assembly of Canada 1841-60. He served as Canada's commissioner of public works 1850-51. A strong proponent of improved canals on the St. Lawrence, Merritt promoted many important projects in the field of transportation.

Erected by the Ontario Archaeological and Historic Sites Board.

John N. Jackson

A St. Catharines' business man, William Hamilton Merritt, acclaimed as the Father of Canadian Transportation, is honoured by this plaque in St. Catharines.

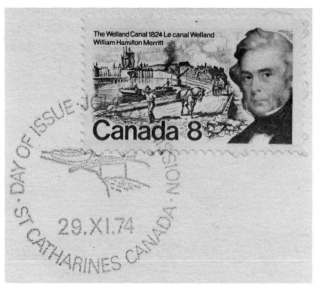

St. Catharines Historical Museum

The initiation of the Welland Canal was commemorated in 1974 by a special stamp.

of the age. For this accomplishment, great regard must be paid to the abilities and prowess of a St. Catharines merchant and mill owner, William Hamilton Merritt. It was he who had the grand concept of achieving a working canal and who strove so desperately for its achievement.

There are also the factors of Canadian sentiment and pride. The Niagara Peninsula had been invaded by U.S. military forces during the War of 1812 and, with the construction of the Erie Canal from Buffalo to Albany across New York State after these hostilities, a clamour arose for a comparable enterprise that would link Lakes Erie and Ontario and take British goods along the St. Lawrence outlet to Montreal.

As Merritt stated when turning the sod for the First Welland Canal at Allanburg in 1824:

"We are assembled here this day for the purpose of removing the first earth from a canal which will, with the least, and by the shortest distance, connect the greatest extent of inland waters, in the whole world.... I verily believe it to be as great a national object to the Province as the Erie Canal to the State of New York.... We will effect the same object for one fiftieth part of the money, and will reap equal if not superior advantages by the Welland."[1]

The Canal, conceived both as the commencement of the St. Lawrence navigations and as the most important link in the chain of communications from inland North America to the Atlantic Ocean, left Lake Ontario at Port Dalhousie. It then followed the valley of Twelve Mile Creek to St. Catharines, climbed the Escarpment via Merritton and Thorold, passed through Allanburg to Port Robinson, and used the Welland River downstream to Chippawa before following the Niagara River upstream to Fort Erie. Opened in 1829, the channel was extended south in 1833 through Welland to Lake Erie at Port Colborne. A direct route had been provided for the first time between Lake Ontario and Lake Erie. These introductory works of the Welland Canal were undertaken not by government, but by the private Welland Canal Company with Merritt at the helm of achievement.

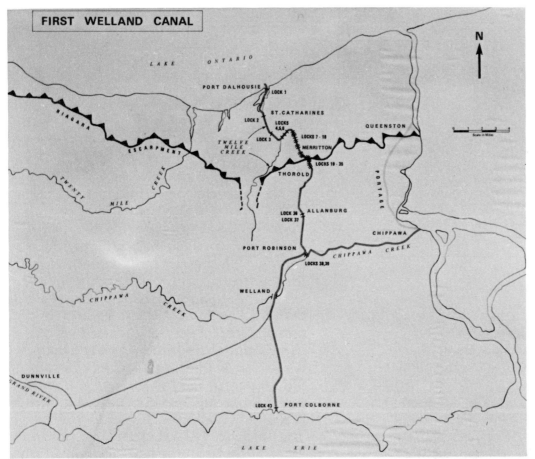

The First Welland Canal, opened in 1829, connected Lake Ontario via Twelve Mile Creek and the Chippawa Creek (Welland River) to the Upper Niagara River and Lake Erie. The Canal was extended south, and opened between Port Robinson and Port Colborne in 1833.

Department of Geography, Brock University

1.2 The Changing Canal System

In 1841 the Welland Canal was purchased from its private shareholders by the government of the new province of Canada. Port Dalhousie was improved as the northern port of entry,

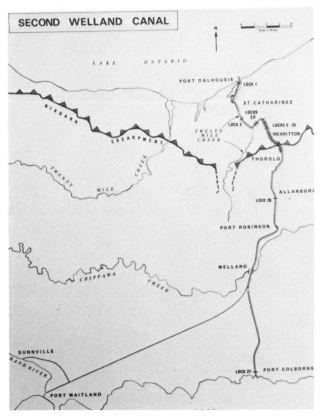

SECOND WELLAND CANAL

Department of Geography, Brock University

The Second Welland Canal, opened in 1845, followed approximately the same route as the First Canal but to higher construction standards. It now had stone not wooden locks.

John Burtniak Collection

The lock of the Second Canal at Port Robinson between the Welland Canal and the Welland River, ca. 1900. Note the detail of the bridge, the lock gates, and the lock-keeper's hut.

meanders in the former channel were eliminated and, with 27 stone locks replacing the original 40 wooden locks, a route slightly to the west was followed across the Escarpment. Southwards, the Second Canal was an enlarged version of its predecessor, with a stone aqueduct now carrying the Canal over the Welland River at Welland. An improved port of entry at Port Colborne, a duplicate entry to the Feeder Canal at Port Robinson, and a lock at Welland to connect the Canal with navigation along the Upper Welland River, were also constructed.

Steamers of larger size were now replacing the small sailing vessels that used the Canal, leading

7

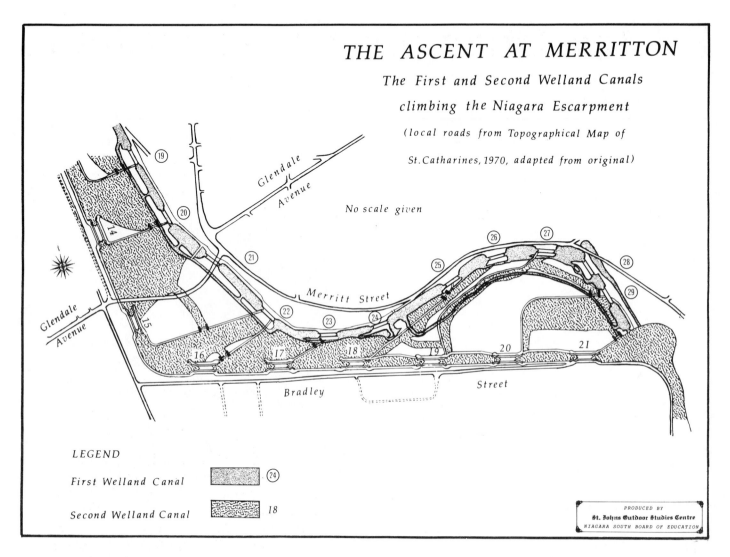

THE ASCENT AT MERRITTON

The First and Second Welland Canals

climbing the Niagara Escarpment

(local roads from Topographical Map of

St. Catharines, 1970, adapted from original)

No scale given

Glendale Avenue

Glendale Avenue

Merritt Street

Bradley Street

LEGEND

First Welland Canal   ⑳

Second Welland Canal   18

PRODUCED BY
St. Johns Outdoor Studies Centre
NIAGARA SOUTH BOARD OF EDUCATION

Colin Duquemin, St. Johns Outdoor Studies Centre

The Second Welland Canal and its water system were located on the left bank of the First Canal where it crossed the Niagara Escarpment between Thorold and Merritton.

to the opening of the Third Canal (its second major reconstruction) in 1887. The entrance harbours of Port Dalhousie and Port Colborne were again enlarged. The locks were reduced in number, increased in size, and placed on a new route from Port Dalhousie to Thorold. The channel south was shortened, but remained via Welland to Port Colborne on Lake Erie. Ships with a draught of 4.26 m (14 feet) could now navigate through the system, which was more than adequate because the downstream St. Lawrence Canals could not pass vessels displacing more than this depth until 1904.

The unrolling saga of expansion and change continued with unabated verve and resulted in the Fourth Canal. The first works to a larger scale included a government grain elevator, larger breakwaters, and deepening the harbour at Port Colborne. A new artificial harbour was constructed on Lake Ontario at Port Weller. The channel with its locks now followed the valley of Ten Mile Creek to the Escarpment, where the

Picturesque Canada, 1882

A stone aqueduct at Welland carried the Second Canal over the Welland River. The County Court House is seen in the background.

The entrance to the Second Canal at Port Dalhousie.

Picturesque Canada, 1882

famous triple series of double flight locks were constructed. Beyond, unnecessary curves were eliminated, and the deepened Canal required that the Welland River be taken under its channel by a syphon culvert. The whole, opened officially in 1932, was taken over by the St. Lawrence Seaway Authority in 1959. The major subsequent change has been the construction of a By-Pass Channel around Welland. This was opened for the 1973 navigation season.

Improvement, change and modification are not features of the distant past. In the mid-1960s, proposals were announced for a new alignment around the City of Welland; these become the Welland Canal By-Pass of 1973. Also announced was the concept of a new route from the Escarpment to Lake Ontario. Land was acquired east of the present channel, with the grandiose idea of *"super-locks"* having a lift of 24.38 m (80 feet) or more to surmount the obstacle of the Niagara Escarpment. Depending on technology, any number from one to four locks could be constructed by the end of this century.

The impressive project of a Fifth Canal, will

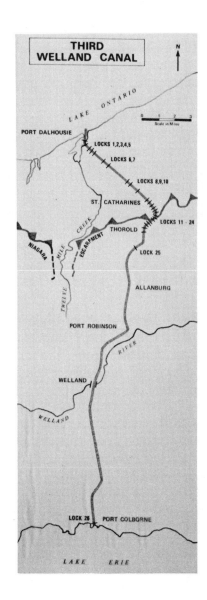

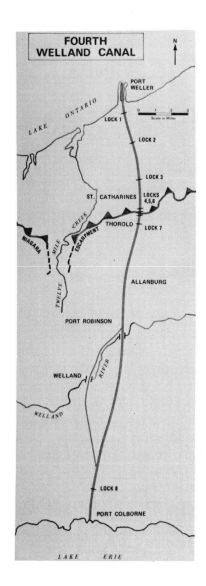

Department of Geography, Brock University

The routes of the Third and Fourth Welland Canals. Note the re-routing of the northern length, and the straighter alignment to the south.

Lock 8 of the Fourth Welland Canal under construction in the late-1920's.

The Fourth Welland Canal through Welland, abandoned as an active waterway in 1973, is now used for recreational activities.

doubtless come to fruition as traffic flows increase. As stated by an Ontario provincial Task Force in 1981: *"The Welland Canal, under present conditions and with the present fleet mix, will not be able to handle the forecasted demand in 1985."* It was recommended that the planning and design of a major enlargement to both the Welland Canal and the Montreal to Lake Ontario Section of the Great Lakes/Seaway System should begin immediately.

The Welland Canal is and always has been in a state of change as the economy, trading patterns and technological abilities continue to progress. Short term improvements are doubtless feasible to increase the tonnage that is handled: a longer navigation season may be practicable; it may become possible for vessels to moor, and to enter and leave locks, at an increased speed; the computerized control of ship movements may be used to decrease the time of passage through the Canal; widening the Canal might assist the two-way movement of ships. In the long term, probably before the end of the century, a complete new Canal system may have to be constructed across the Niagara landscape.

Welland Ship Canal. Excavation in Site Welland South Dock, looking S. 7C4 Aug 25/32.

The continuing saga of new construction typifies the Canal scene. Depicted are excavations for the Fourth Canal in Welland South during 1932.

FIRST WELLAND CANAL

STARTED 1824 —— COMPLETED 1829

TYPICAL VESSEL

LENGTH 100 FT. – CARGO CAPACITY 165 TONS

TYPICAL LOCK

LENGTH BETWEEN GATES _ _ _ _ _ _ _110 FT.
WIDTH OF LOCK _ _ _ _ _ _ _ _ _ _ _ 22 FT.
DEPTH OF WATER OVER SILLS _ _ _ _ _8 FT.
SINGLE LIFTS _ _ _ _ _ _ _ _ _ 6FT. _TO_ 11 FT.
NUMBER OF LOCKS _ _ _ _ _ _ _ _ _ _ _39

SECOND WELLAND CANAL

STARTED 1842 —— COMPLETED 1845

TYPICAL VESSEL

LENGTH 140 FT. – CARGO CAPACITY 750 TONS

TYPICAL LOCK

LENGTH BETWEEN GATES _ _ _ _ _ _ _150 FT.
WIDTH OF LOCK _ _ _ _ _ _ _ _ _ _ 26 FT. 6 IN.
DEPTH OF WATER OVER SILLS _ _ _ _ _ 9 FT.
SINGLE LIFTS _ _ _ _ _ 9FT. 6IN. TO 14FT.3IN.
NUMBER OF LOCKS _ _ _ _ _ _ _ _ _ _ _27

THIRD WELLAND CANAL

STARTED 1875 —— COMPLETED 1887

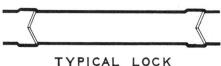

TYPICAL VESSEL

LENGTH 255 FT. – CARGO CAPACITY 2700 TONS

TYPICAL LOCK

LENGTH BETWEEN GATES _ _ _ _ _ _270 FT.
WIDTH OF LOCK _ _ _ _ _ _ _ _ _ _ _ 45 FT.
DEPTH OF WATER OVER SILLS _ _ _ _ _14 FT.
SINGLE .LIFTS _ _ _ _ _ _ _ _ _ 12FT. TO 16 FT.
NUMBER OF LOCKS _ _ _ _ _ _ _ _ _ _ _26

P. J. Cowan, The Welland Ship Canal, 1935

The changing size of Canal locks and vessels.

1.3 The Channel and Its Harbours

The Canal, as an engineering construct to overcome differences in level from Lake Erie to Lake Ontario, has a surface width of flowing water. Its *"prism"*, or cross section, has a width at the bottom and an angle of slope for its banks, which together dictate the size of the vessels that can be used on the Canal. This argument can be reversed—given the expected size of vessels in terms of their length, breadth and depth, then these dimensions control the size of the Canal. Channel dimensions on the modern Welland Canal are generally 59 m (192 feet) for the width of the bottom and 94 m (310 feet) for the width of the water surface, increasing to 107 m (350 feet) and 152 m (500 feet) for the Welland By-Pass. The depth of the prism is generally 8.2 m (27 feet).

As the channel must be watertight, the Canal is *"puddled"* or layered with clay along the base and sides. To prevent the erosion of banks by the wash from passing boats, the banks at the water line are lined with stone for protective purposes. The speed of passing vessels is also restricted, to 7.7 knots (9 miles per hour) over the bottom through the Welland By-Pass, and elsewhere to 6.1 knots (7 miles per hour).

The channel takes on many forms. It is generally a *"ditch"* or *"cut"* in the land surface, but it may be raised above adjacent ground on an embankment or be in an aqueduct when it

St. Lawrence Seaway Authority

The prism or cross-section of the modern Canal as seen when drained for winter maintenance.

Fred A. Addis

The Canal and its structures control the size and shape of ships.

crosses a transverse stream. River improvement may also be involved. Each type of channel has been incorporated in the evolving Welland Canal System.

The First and Second Canals included a length of Twelve Mile Creek, and its tributary at St. Catharines (Dick's Creek), as part of their effective routes. With the construction of the Third Canal, the channel became wholly a man-made achievement. On the modern system the channel generally occupies a cut in the landscape, an exception being parts of the northern length between the Queen Elizabeth Way and Lake Ontario where it is on a raised embankment. Lock 2 (Carlton Street) is higher than its neighbouring terrain. An aqueduct took the First, Second and Third Canals over the Welland River at Welland; that of the Second Canal survives in use as an open-air swimming pool in downtown Welland.

The channel also extends into Lake Ontario and Lake Erie at the two ends of the Canal; it is then gouged into the beds of the respective Lakes and protected from wind and current by breakwaters. Port Colborne is the deeper entrance; its controlling depth is 9.1 m (30 feet), which contrasts with 8.2 m (27 feet) at Port Weller.

Port Weller Harbour is wholly man-made. As such it may be compared with Port Colborne, or contrasted with its predecessor at Port Dalhousie. The latter harbour began as a lake ponded in the valley of Twelve Mile Creek behind a lakeshore sand bar. All the surviving harbour entrances are enclosed by protective breakwaters: two arms at Port Dalhousie, pincer- or prong-shaped and longer at Port Weller, and with greatly enlarged

St. Lawrence Seaway Authority
Widening the Deep Cut between Allanburg and Port Robinson.

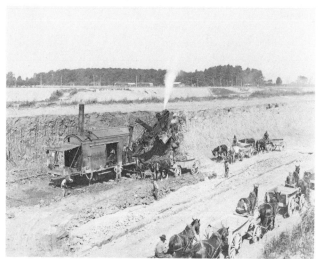

Fred Campbell Collection
Steam shovel loading mule-driven wagons.

Excavating the channel, a contrast in techniques, 1930 (right) and 1980 (left).

16

P.J Cowan, The Welland Ship Canal, 1935
The Canal as creator of landscape. Constructing the west arm of Port Weller Harbour in 1914.

John N. Jackson
A man-made projection into Lake Ontario, the Port Weller entrance.

banks and breakwaters parallel to the shore at Port Colborne. Each harbour entrance has thereby taken on its own distinctive character.

Wharves, numbered 1 to 19 from north to south along the Canal, are located in the major urban centres. Their most recent member (wharf 10) is on the west bank of the By-Pass Channel at Welland. An extensive sequence of wharves line the channel continuously through Port Colborne.

When a channel is cut, the *"spoil"* or material removed from the excavations has to be deposited somewhere, a process which in turn creates new canalscape features. Low spoil hills are located at the side of the channel north of Welland along the Fourth Canal, and on both banks of the By-Pass Channel. Rock materials excavated from the northern length of channel and the site of the flight locks were used to create the breakwaters that enclose the dredged channel and harbour at Port Weller.

The channel, whether cut into terrain or on an

17

embankment, may interfere with the natural flow of drainage, curtail transverse streams, reduce their flow, and hold back their upper waters. In this respect, a critical difference exists between the northern and the southern sections of the Canal.

In the north, where the land slopes gently from the base of the Escarpment to the bluffs of Lake Ontario, the modern Canal has been constructed in the former valley of Ten Mile Creek. Natural drainage is from south to north, the Canal is in accord with these conditions, and does not intersect existing streams.

The situation is very different south of the Niagara Escarpment. The Canal is now at right angles to the topographic detail. It cuts through the low ridge between Allanburg and Port Robinson in the Deep Cut. The head waters of several smaller streams have been severed by the Canal, and the Welland River is taken under the By-Pass Channel by an inverted syphon culvert. Ponding caused by the Canal is best observed on its east bank to the south of the Thorold Tunnel.

1.4 Water Flow and Supply

Canals require an adequate and regular supply of water that is sufficient for navigation in the driest of seasons. This source must be higher than the *"summit level"* or highest point of the Canal, and also of sufficient flow to offset the loss of water from the Canal through its locks, evaporation and seepage. This supply of water for the Welland Canal was obtained from the Grand River by way of the Feeder Canal from Dunnville to Welland from its inception in 1829 until 1881, when Lake Erie at Port Colborne became and has remained the source of supply. Lake Erie is now the *"head pond"* for the Canal, and water flows north through the Canal from Port Colborne to Port Weller.

Picturesque Canada, 1882

A waste weir and lock at Thorold on the Second Canal.

St. Lawrence Seaway Authority

A waste weir undergoing repair.

Water must be controlled for entry into the total system and along its various lengths; otherwise, without this regulation, it might overflow the banks. Waste weirs, or pipes in the bed controlled by valves, are therefore installed to discharge surplus water to lower ground. Guard gates are also necessary for, should the lock gates be breached, an extensive length of canal would otherwise be drained of water; also, a canal has sometimes to be drained of water in order to permit the continuing process of repair and maintenance to its banks and beds.

On the modern Canal, its flow of water from Lake Erie is controlled by a supply weir at Port Colborne across the raceway or former channel of the Third Canal. There is also a protective guard or regulating lock (Lock 8) on the present channel, its purpose being to maintain a consistent level of water in the Canal irrespective of fluctuations in the level of Lake Erie. In addition, a guard gate is located south of Lock 7 at the crest of the Escarpment. This gate, when closed, allows the northern length of the Canal to be drained for winter repair and maintenance works, though certain reaches can be drained with or without the guard gate.

The total flow of water now entering the Canal at Port Colborne can be as high as 300 cubic metres (m^3) per second (1 m^3 = 1000 litres. .7646 m^3 per second = 27 cubic feet per second (cfs).) Probably a surprise to most readers is that only a small proportion of this flow, approximately 10 to 15 percent, is used to lower ships from Lake Erie to Lake Ontario on their downbound transit or to lift upbound traffic through the 100 metres (326 feet) of vertical distance. Whenever a vessel is lowered in a lock, nearly 100,000 m^3 (21,000,000 gallons) of water are *"dumped"*, or spilled, into the reach below. Fortunately the same water is used again at the next lower lock, and so on until it is finally dumped into Lake Ontario. The water used for lockages and water level control depends on the volume of ship traffic through the Canal and, during the busy summer months, the average flow can be as high as 40 m^3/sec. In addition another 10 m^3/sec. of water is used by the Seaway's powerhouse located below the Flight Locks to generate electricity for use on the Canal system.

The greatest amount of flow is used for other than Canal purposes. Ontario Hydro is by far the largest user, diverting about 200 m^3/sec. from the Canal to the DeCew Power Plant on Twelve Mile Creek in South St. Catharines. The local municipalities of Welland, Thorold and St. Catharines also rely on the Canal to supply approximately 6 m^3/sec. of water for domestic purposes.

Water for the DeCew Power Plant and the DeCew Water Filtration Plant in St. Catharines is taken from the Canal at Allanburg. It feeds the extensive lake complex from Beaverdams to DeCew just south of the Escarpment edge. These lakes, used for local recreational and fishing purposes, drain into Twelve Mile Creek and considerably augment its water flow. Walking, cycle and fitness trails in the valley bottom from DeCew to Port Dalhousie, and the water levels of Martindale Pond, each benefit from this augmented water.

John N. Jackson

Water is diverted from the Welland Canal at Allanburg to serve the DeCew hydro-electric plant.

Water is also taken from the abandoned and operative lengths of the Canal to serve industry. A total of about 4 m³/sec. is used to help in the production of items that range from steel to farm equipment, and from engines to newsprint and fine paper, by well-known regional firms such as Atlas Steels, John Deere, Union Carbide, Stelco, Ontario Paper, Exolon, General Motors, Kimberly-Clark, Domtar, Beaverwood and Hayes Dana. The abandoned Second Canal through Thorold and St. Catharines, and the abandoned Third Canal north of the Escarpment, are also fed from the present Canal.

Another 20 m³/sec. of water is used to create flows to prevent stagnation and to provide dilu-

tion in Lyons Creek and the Welland River. Minor uses include some summer-time irrigation of farm lands, and moving vessels in and out of the Port Weller Dry Docks for repairs and inspection work.

John N. Jackson

The Canal as a channel of water, looking north from Glendale Bridge, St. Catharines, to where the Third Canal (right) crosses the line of the present Canal. Lock 3 is top left.

As water commitments from the Canal are year round, only the northern length of the Canal can be de-watered during the winter season of no navigation. As the water level is lowered, objects such as abandoned cars come into view. Winter is the best season to view the massive size of the flight locks and their impressive gates. With no water in the Canal their full dimensions are then most apparent.

At Welland, a proportion of the water flowing in the By-Pass Channel is diverted south into the abandoned channel, where it is used for dilution purposes and to serve the Welland waterworks. This water, completing a circular tour, then feeds into the Welland River and passes back under the Canal in a syphon culvert at Welland.

Water in the Canal has always and still does provide an important recreational amenity. A ribbon of water, wider than most rivers, has been introduced across the Niagara Peninsula. As the banks of the Canal are frequently landscaped with mature trees, and as vehicular access is available to most lengths of the Canal, visitors are regularly attracted to the scene with its passing ships. A parkway along the length of the Canal, a feasible proposition because an almost continuous road exists along the full length of the Canal, has been mooted on several past occasions but not achieved. Advantage could certainly be taken of the colourful and changing Canal scene to provide a facility in like vein to the Niagara River Parkway along the Niagara River. This would interlink the various features of canalscape that are discussed in this text.

1.5 The Locks

Locks on the Welland Canal are essentially *"chambers"* with gates at each end. These gates meet in the centre at a *"mitre"* angle of some 135 degrees to better resist the pressure of water. Vessels are raised or lowered by changing the water-level in a lock. They are in effect transferred from one *"reach"* or *"pond"* of the Canal to another, a reach being the stretch of water between two locks and the *"lift"* of a lock being the difference in height between two adjoining reaches. Tie-up walls are located above and below each independent lock and at either end of the flight locks. Ships moor here for short periods whilst awaiting passage through the locks.

For a vessel to ascend, the upper gates and sluices that command the flow of water from the upper reach are closed. The ship enters the lock from the lower reach; the lower gates are then closed and the valves are opened. As water flows into the lock by gravity from the upper reach, the water rising in the lock brings the ship up to the upper level. When this is attained the valves are closed, the upper gates are opened and the ship moves from the lock into the upper reach of the canal. These stages are reversed when a vessel is lowered from one level to another. Seven locks, with lifts of 14.6 m (47.9 feet), and one guard lock, take vessels through the Canal.

Locks have to cope with excess water from the upper level; at times some water may flow over the gates, but most of the excess is diverted through waste weirs located at the side of the lock. The size and form of locks have changed

St. Lawrence Seaway Authority

The unwatered chamber of Lock 1 showing winter maintenance in progress. Note the water supply portals at the base of each lock wall.

considerably through time. They began as wooden structures, then stone, and are now lined with concrete. Gates, first of oak, are now of steel. Opening and closing operations have

23

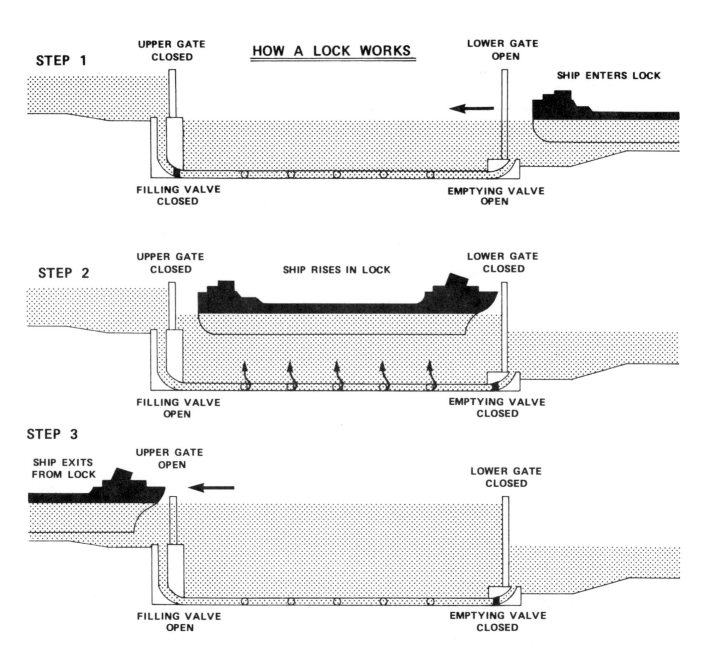

HOW A LOCK WORKS

STEP 1

UPPER GATE CLOSED

LOWER GATE OPEN

SHIP ENTERS LOCK

FILLING VALVE CLOSED

EMPTYING VALVE OPEN

STEP 2

UPPER GATE CLOSED

SHIP RISES IN LOCK

LOWER GATE CLOSED

FILLING VALVE OPEN

EMPTYING VALVE CLOSED

STEP 3

SHIP EXITS FROM LOCK

UPPER GATE OPEN

LOWER GATE CLOSED

FILLING VALVE OPEN

EMPTYING VALVE CLOSED

Department of Geography, Brock University

Water enters the lock from portals at the base of each wall, raising the ship as in a tank when the gates are closed. The situation is reversed when the vessel is lowered.

changed from hand to mechanical means. The lock chamber has become broader, longer and deeper to accommodate larger vessels. Locks were at first always separated from their neighbours by reaches of canal and, to save water, side ponds or storage reservoirs were added above each lock. This situation prevailed on the First, Second and Third Canals.

John N. Jackson

Upbound (right) and downbound (left) ships passing in the Flight Locks. Note the difference in levels between the two ships.

Locks were first placed together in *"flights"* to overcome substantial differences in level when the Fourth Canal was constructed, with the upper gate of the lower lock now also being the lower gate of the upper lock. As this lock sequence was also twinned with a double set of locks side by side of the other, vessels no longer have to await the passage of ships in the other direction at these points. A flight of locks saves on vessel time over passing through a series of separated locks. It economizes on the use of water but, the larger the locks and the greater their use, the greater is the volume of water that must pass through the Canal.

Locks do not provide the only solution for overcoming obstacles of relief. In earlier days, and as intended though not achieved on the First Canal, methods other than locks were considered to overcome height differences. The Welland proposal was for a railway incline at DeCew Falls. A slope can be overcome by using capstans, placing boats on rollers, and through using the counterbalancing weight of the descending boat to raise the ascending vessel. The boat can be placed in a wheeled trolley running on rails, as at Big Chute on the Trent Canal. A hydraulic vertical-lift lock using an enclosed, water-tight tank might be used, as in the Cohinoor Lock at Peterborough and at Kirkfield. Many variances are possible. Ingenuity in the circumstances of the day, including both technology and the availability of funds, must be the hall-mark of every canal engineer.

Vessels have to be manoeuvered in the canal. Because of the narrow dimensions, sail was impracticable in the early days. Haulage by horse or mule power was favoured initially, which required a tow path, animal storage and feeding

J.D. Barnes Limited, Toronto, from
University Map Library, Department of
Geography, Brock University

The Flight Locks (Locks 4,5 and 6) and Lock 7 in their urban setting, 1974. Thorold to the left, Third Canal locks and weirs top right.

services, and formal arrangements for passing when two vessels under tow met in the channel. As an example, the tow path of the Second Canal was on the west bank across the Escarpment, with pondage and weirs on the east bank. As the latter attracted industry to an available source of power, industry located primarily on the east bank of the original Canal system. This side of the Canal was strengthened for industrial location, when the north-south Welland Railway followed the east bank from Port Dalhousie to Port Colborne in the 1850s.

The speed of movement for vessels through the Canal was at first slow, being about two miles an hour through the reaches until tow animals were replaced by the steam tug boat from about the 1850s. The tug, however, posed a new set of problems: it took up vital space in the locks, and greater speed and bulk increased wash along the banks. Eventually, self propulsion by vessels using the Canal became the norm.

1.6 Bridges and Crossings

Bridges have necessarily crossed the Canal since its inception, being important where the Canal severed east-west road connections and when settlements grew next to the Canal. Locks have always provided a favoured site, because here the width of water to be spanned was at its narrowest, and the lock or its approaches could be used as the base for the bridge. Railways, with their heavier loads, introduced stronger bridges and the powered opening span. Crossings of the modern Canal indicate strongly both changing technology and changing demands for land crossings, with movable structures gradually giving way to a fewer number of fixed bridges and tunnels.

Twenty movable bridges were constructed over the Fourth Canal—seven bascule or rolling-lift bridges, with five having a single leaf, one a double leaf (No. 4 at Homer), and one with two separated single spans (No. 6 at the Flight Locks); 11 vertical-lift bridges; and two swing bridges. Like the locks, they are numbered sequentially from north to south. Bridge 1 is on Lakeshore Road in St. Catharines and Bridge 21 on Clarence Street in Port Colborne. Bridge No. 2 was not constructed but, as the intent was not abandoned until a late date of Canal construction, it is included in the numbered sequence. The numbers are now incomplete because some bridges have been taken out of service; others, with an **"A"** suffix to the number, have been added so that 11 movable highway and/or railway bridges now cross the Canal. They include five vertical-lift, five single leaf rolling bascule,

and one double leaf rolling bascule bridge.

The swing bridges were constructed before World War I. Neither is operative today. Bridge 8, which took the **Niagara, St. Catharines and Toronto** electric street railway over the Canal in Thorold, was removed when the inter-city trolley system succumbed to road traffic. Bridge 15, taking track of the **Michigan Central** and **Toronto, Hamilton and Buffalo** over the Canal near downtown Welland, posed a navigational hazard with its central pier within the Canal and was a factor in the need for a By-Pass Channel at Welland; it remains, but in a fixed position over the abandoned channel.

Except at Bridge 4 on Queenston Street in St. Catharines, the bascule bridges are associated with lock approach walls where the channel is narrow. They are to be found north of the Escarpment and at Port Colborne, including the new structure of Bridge 19A opened in 1981 to relieve traffic congestion on Highway 3. These bridges lift with a counterweight framework rolling back into teeth on fixed track built into the concrete substructure. They are most visible when the leaf or leaves are raised for passing ships.

The vertical-lift bridge may be regarded as the **"typical"** Canal bridge. A line of such bridges marks the southern length of the original Fourth Canal, and one (Bridge 5) is located north of the Escarpment. They are visually prominent in the landscape, especially when in a raised position to permit the passage of ships. The twin latticed towers are 50.29 m (165 feet) high; cables and counterweights move up and

St. Lawrence Seaway Authority

John N. Jackson

Movable bridges were constructed over the Fourth Canal.
A rolling-lift bridge at Homer and

a vertical-lift bridge at Welland

Fred A. Addis

Fred A. Addis

Vertical-lift bridges take Clarence Street and the Canadian National tracks across the Fourth Canal in Port Colborne, a land and an air view.

Five vertical-lift bridges survive along the abandoned channel in Welland. Anchored in a permanent down position since the By-Pass Channel opened in 1973, their most commanding representative is former Bridge 13 that dominates and gives character to the main street of Downtown Welland. Bridge 12 at Port Robinson was ignominiously destroyed in 1974 when a downbound ship struck the span, and toppled both towers; it has been replaced by a seasonal ferry, which carries only passengers. Bridge 21 also provides a vital feature next to the core of Downtown Port Colborne.

All movable bridges are operated by electric motors capable of opening them to their full extent in approximately 1.5 minutes. Diesel standby engines are provided should power failure occur. The free-standing bridges are operated by a Bridgemaster located on the structure, with controls and an interlock system to prevent accidents. Bridges adjacent to locks are operated remotely from the lock control room.

All bridges are equipped with navigation signal lights, red indicating that the bridge is closed or in motion, and green indicating that the bridge is fully open for navigation. Whistle posts, caution signs, and limit of approach signs are used to control the approach of a vessel and the bridge operation. As shipping normally takes precedence over vehicular or rail traffic, the bridges are points of delay on the highway system. It requires approximately 10 minutes to pass a vessel through a bridge *"draw"*, i.e. from bridge lowered, to raised, to lowered.

Movable bridges were designed to suit the traffic volumes of the 1930s. They then caused no great inconvenience to road traffic but, with

down in these towers. A machinery house and operating room are located centrally on top of the lift span. The span, when fully raised, provides a clearance of 36.6 m (120 feet) above water level; the masts of vessels must not extend more than 35.5 metres (116.5 feet) above water level.

30

priority awarded to shipping movements, the frustration of traffic congestion on major highway routes, increasing traffic volumes and new road construction have led to the provision of fixed crossings over or under the Canal that do not hinder the flow of traffic.

John N. Jackson

As road traffic increased, the Garden City Skyway (foreground) replaced the twin rolling-lift bridge on former Highway 8.

The high level Burgoyne Bridge has crossed the channel of the Second Canal in St. Catharines to connect the downtown area with the main line railway station since World War I. This was the only such structure over the earlier Canals. Its modern equivalent, carrying major east-west highway flows over the Canal, is the Garden City Skyway at St. Catharines. Opened in 1963, it takes six traffic lanes of the Queen Elizabeth Way over the Canal on a spectacular curving structure. The bridge rises to 37.5 m (123 feet) above the Canal, it is approximately 2,130 m (7,000 feet) long, there are some 3.2 kilometres (two miles) of approaches, and over

80 supporting columns. This gargantuan crossing of the Canal radically changed the townscape characteristics of north St. Catharines.

The remaining crossings, as tunnels under the Canal, are more secreted within the landscape. The Thorold Tunnel, opened in 1968, replaced

John N. Jackson

The highway and highway-rail tunnels under the By-Pass Channel at East Main Street (above) and Townline Road (below), Welland.

John N. Jackson

two bascule lift-bridges for highway traffic. Three features are of interest: it was constructed in the dry over three winters when the Canal was de-watered; its two tubes each carry two traffic lanes; and the architecturally-designed flared approaches offset the sudden transition from light to dark on the eyes of drivers.

The Welland Canal By-Pass, opened in 1973, included two tunnels as part of the contractual arrangements. The East Main Street Tunnel carries four highway lanes on the principal east-west road across the city. It has a 6 percent grade on its approach and is shorter than the Thorold Tunnel, a combination which makes it possible to photograph ocean-going vessels crossing a highway—an unusual world scene to say the least. This is also possible on the approaches to the Townline Tunnel, which carries three lines of rail track to the south at a grade of 0.75 percent and a two-lane highway for vehicles to the north at a grade of 4 percent. All tunnels have concrete roofs, then a minimum of rip-rap. The hydrographic chart tactfully recommends ***"that anchors not be dropped in these areas!"***

These fixed bridges and tunnels can incorporate pipes and conduits that accommodate public utilities. In addition, overhead cables cross the Canal over parts of its southern length, reflecting hydro-electric power developments at

St. Lawrence Seaway Authority

Bridge 19A at Port Colborne, the most recent bridge over the Canal, was opened in 1981 to relieve traffic congestion on Highway 3.

the Falls and the grid of its long-distance transmission system. High level cables are taken over the Welland By-Pass by special pylons, providing a clearance of 43 m (140 feet) over the Canal for the high voltage cables; the pylons are among the highest ever constructed by Ontario Hydro. As various submerged utility cables and pipelines are also taken under the Canal, the Canal is now more of a perceived than an actual barrier to urban expansion.

1.7 An Industrial Catalyst

William Hamilton Merritt, at the inaugural ceremony of 1824, recognized that the Canal would create new industrial opportunities:

"This canal, from its peculiar and most favourable situation, will be the means of creating within itself, or by its own erection, a greater amount of transportation than will pay the interest of the capital expended, over and above the transit it will draw from Lake Erie, and the profits of its hydraulic situation.... This canal ... will afford the best and most numerous situations for machinery, within the same distance in America; wet or dry, warm or cold, we always have the same abundant and steady supply of water.... A general tide of prosperity will be witnessed on the whole line and surrounding country."

John Burtniak Collection

John N. Jackson

John N. Jackson

The Canal attracted industry to its banks. Atlas Steels in Welland (left), the REO plant in St. Catharines which produced the first automobile to cross Canada (above), and the pulp and paper industry of St. Catharines-Thorold (below).

33

Such prognostications were correct. The Canal nurtured industry. It became a catalyst, creating a line of settlement across the landscape of the Niagara Peninsula. This impact of the Canal included many business and industrial enterprises, mills, factories and homes which together fostered urban growth and regional evolution. This impact continues; the Canal is both of the past, and of today and tomorrow. It is an expression of development *in* the landscape, and a powerful medium of change *on* that landscape.

Construction works caused the immigration of labour. These workers had to be fed and housed. Their wages circulated back into the local economy, as did expenditures by the Welland Canal Company, ship owners, and the crews of vessels. Administrative offices, toll collection points and customs had to be established. Commodities carried on the ships provided a basis for industrial development. The import of raw materials and the export of products were assisted. Water from the Canal was available to drive machinery, to develop power, and for use in industrial processes. It could be diverted from the Canal into raceways to serve activities that were not on its banks. Points where the Canal were crossed by road and rail communications became focal points on the communications' network. Wharves, docks and harbours along the Canal attracted warehouses, industries, service activities and the outdoor storage of materials. The economy of the Niagara Peninsla

John N. Jackson

Industry formerly lined the Canal bank north of Burgoyne Bridge, St. Catharines.

John Burtniak Collection

The largest early shipbuilding enterprise was the Shickluna Shipyard in St. Catharines.

Ontario Paper Company

The Ontario Paper Company located on the Third Welland Canal at Thorold in 1912, to become the fifth largest producer of newsprint in North America. It manufactures ethyl alcohol, salt cake and vanillin, and completed a $260 million modernization and expansion in 1982.

Robin Brown, STELCO
STELCO, a major canal-oriented industry, Welland.

was thereby changed radically by the assertive presence of the Welland Canal.

Industry has always been associated with the Canal. Mills took immediate advantage of its water power. By 1847, they were grouped on sites at Dunnville, Wainfleet, Port Robinson, Allanburg, Thorold and St. Catharines, producing domestic goods, flour, timber, cloth and metal items. Prominent industrial survivals with Canal associations include Lincoln Fabrics at Port Dalhousie, Barnes Wines near the Queen Elizabeth Way, Canada Hair Cloth next to downtown St. Catharines, and a line of industry from Merritton across the crest of the Escarpment into and through Thorold. Paper plants such as Abitibi-Price, Domtar, Kimberly-Clark, Beaver Wood Fibre, and Ontario Paper each have sites of Canal importance. Hayes Dana, two plants of General Motors and the Port Weller Dry Docks should be added to this imposing list of major industry. A second Hayes Dana plant is located on the Canal south of Thorold. In Welland, Atlas Steels, John Deere, the Page Hersey and Welland Tube Works of the Steel Company of Canada and Union Carbide testify to the ongoing role of the waterway. In Port Colborne, the grouping of Canal-related industries includes ship repair and servicing, steel works, nickel refining, grain elevators, and the handling and processing of bulk materials.

1.8 A Chain of Urban Settlement

Industry and commercial activities create cities which survive and prosper, even though they are no longer associated directly with the active waterway. Their citizens forget the importance of the Canal for their very existence. For example, the Feeder Canal that initiated Dunnville and villages on route to Welland, fell gradually into disuse and decay after 1881 when the Canal was supplied with water from Lake Erie. The Third Canal removed through shipping activity from the downtown areas of Thorold and St. Catharines in the 1880s, the Fourth Canal deserted Port Dalhousie as the northern port of entry in the 1960s, and the By-Pass Channel of the early 1970s took the Fourth Canal out of the core of Welland. Allanburg and Port Robinson, as elsewhere, have gradually been divested of their Canal functions and buildings, through channel widening and relocation, and as larger-sized, self-propelled vessels no longer required services

Ontario Archives S5878, from
St. Catharines Historical Museum.

St. Catharines changed from a village to an industrial town and became a city because of its location next to the Welland Canal. Note the hydraulic raceway on the Canal bank in this scene, ca. 1920.

MAIN LINE

PORT DALHOUSIE

The entrance of the Welland Canal from Lake Ontario. A harbour has been formed, having a basin of 500 acres in extent, with a depth of water of from twelve to sixteen feet. There is a village on the east side of the canal, in the township of Grantham, five miles from St. Catharines, where there is a shipyard. Port Dalhousie contains about 200 inhabitants, two stores, one tavern, two blacksmiths.

ST. CATHARINES

A Town in the township of Grantham, situated on the Welland Canal, thirty-six miles from Hamilton, and twelve miles from Niagara. The town is beautifully situated, having a fine view for a considerble distance of the Welland Canal and surrounding country. It is a place of much trade. . .

THOROLD

A Village in the township of Thorold, situated on the summit of the mountain, four miles from St. Catharines. It was commenced in the year 1826, and now contains about 1000 inhabitants. The Welland Canal runs close past the village. There are three churches and chapels in Thorold, viz., Episcopal, Catholic, and Methodist.

Post Office, post three times a week.

Professions and Trades - Two physicians and surgeons, two grist mills, (one do. in progress), one cement mill, one brewery, nine stores, seven taverns, one tannery, one saddler, one chemist and druggist, three waggon makers, three blacksmiths, two painters, two cabinet makers, two tinsmiths, eight shoemakers, one baker, hatter, two barbers, three tailors, one ladies' school.

ALLENBURG (now Allanburg)

A Village in the township of Thorold, situated on the Welland Canal, 8 miles from St. Catharines. It possesses a town-hall for public meetings.

Population about 500.

Professions and Trades - One grist mill, one saw ditto, carding machine and cloth factory, candle factory, pipe factory, four stores, two taverns, one waggon maker, one cabinet maker, one blacksmith and one baker.

PORT ROBINSON

A Village in the township of Thorold, situated on the Welland Canal, ten miles from St. Catharines. This place is the "head quarters" of the coloured company employed for the maintenance of order on the canal. There are two churches in the village, Episcopal and Presbyterian.

Population, about 300.

Post Office, post three times a week.

Professions and Trades - One grist mill, three stores, three taverns, one saddler, one baker, three groceries, two waggon makers, one watchmaker, two blacksmiths, one tinsmith, three tailors, two shoemakers.

MERRITTSVILLE (now Welland)

A small Settlement in the township of Crowland, one mile and a half from the junction. At this place an aqueduct has been constructed to convey the Welland Canal over the Welland or Chippawa River, the level of the canal being here forty feet above the surface of the river. Merrittsville contains about 100 inhabitants, five stores, three taverns, two tailors, two shoemakers.

STONEBRIDGE, or PETERSBURGH

A Village in the township of Humberstone, situated on the feeder (?) of the Welland Canal, one mile and a half from Lake Erie. It is supported almost entirely by the works on the Canal. A detachment of the Coloured Company is quartered here.

Population about 200, exclusive of the laboures (sic) on the canal

Professions and Trades - One physician and surgeon, one distillery, one foundry, seven stores, one druggist, three taverns, two waggon makers, three blacksmiths, three butchers, four shoemakers, two saddlers, three tailors, one tinsmith.

PORT COLBORNE

A Village in the Township of Humberstone, situated on Lake Erie, at the mouth of the feeder (?) of the Welland Canal; it is a port of entry, and has a resident collector of customs. Population about 150.

Post office, post three times a week.

Professions and Trades - Steam grist mill (not at present in operation), one store, three taverns, one baker, one grocery, one shoemaker.

FEEDER

DUNNVILLE

A Village in the township of Moulton, situated on the Grand River, at its junction with the feeder of the Welland Canal, four miles and three quarters from Lake Erie. It commenced settling in 1829, and now contains about 400 inhabitants. A steam boat plies here regularly during the season, and a smaller boat continues the route to Brantford. Considerable quantities of lumber are shipped here. Dunnville contains an Episcopal church and a Presbyterian church is in progress.

Post Office, post three times a week.

Professions and Trades - One physician and surgeon, two grist mills, three saw mills, one distillery, one Tannery, one carding machine and cloth factory, six stores, four taverns, four groceries, two waggon makers, four blacksmiths, one saddler, two tinsmiths, four shoemakers, three tailors, two cabinet makers, one baker, one turner.

MARSHVILLE (now Wainfleet)

A small Village in the township of Wainfleet, situated on the Grand River feeder of the Welland Canal, ten miles from Port Colborne. It contains about sixty inhabitants, grist mill, two stores, one tavern, one blacksmith.

Post Office, post three times a week.

Retyped from **Smiths Canadian Gazelteer,** 1846.

The settlements which had developed along the Canal by 1846 are described in these excerpts.

within the Canal. Alone of the Canal communities, and though much amended by successive change, only Port Colborne persists astride the shipping artery that provided the essential raison d'être for its existence.

St. Catharines was transformed by the Welland Canal. It was changed from a rural service centre to an industrial town and soon became the paramount city of the Niagara Peninsula because of the Canal. The main street, St. Paul, backed onto the Canal on its southern side, and a line of industry was attracted to this Canal valley and its attendant hydraulic raceways along the north side at various levels. In 1981, this commercial front door of the city is occupied by stores that face St. Paul Street. As a key part of the city's downtown core, it will again become highly visible when a four-lane provincial highway is completed in the valley bottom. A scheme prepared in 1981 by a team from the Ontario Association of Architects and promoted by the St. Catharines Downtown Association provides some hope that civic design, rather than solely highway engineering considerations, will prevail.

Port Dalhousie was not closed to lake shipping until the late 1960s. The inner harbour has taken on a robust activity as the home of the Henley Rowing Regatta, acclaimed as a sporting event of international renown. The outer harbour remains in active use behind protective breakwaters that still project into Lake Ontario. Connecting steamers brought in summer visitors from Toronto to Lakeside Park and transferred others to the streetcar for a journey to Niagara Falls; this summer recreation on the beach survives. More recently, marina facilities for yachts and power boats have taken over these former Canal waters. This ongoing vitality of an active marine scene has promoted the renewal of buildings facing the harbour by local initiative. *"The Port"* has changed from a vigorous if not boisterous port of entry to an attractive residential *"village"*, with numerous historical buildings of character reflecting 150 years of association with the First, Second and Third Canals.

Merritton, formerly an independent community but now part of the City of St. Catharines, is another Canal-fostered centre. It grew where the Canal was crossed by the main **Great Western** (now **Canadian National**) railway line, and because of an abundance of water power from the Canal. The line of industry between Merritton and Thorold still suggests the pre-eminence of this locale for industrial location and expansion during the mid- and late-nineteenth and early twentieth centuries.

Downtown Thorold, wholly a creation of the Canal, grew astride the First and Second Canals. Here, in the *"Mountain City"*, is the true climax

John Burtniak Collection
Port Dalhousie, port of entry to the first three Welland Canals.

39

of the Canal. Now covered over, the former Canal routes are lined with industrial and other buildings, including the Welland Mills of 1846 and the home of John Keefer, once President of the Welland Canal Company.

Fred Campbell Collection

Fred Campbell Collection

Thorold was born and nurtured by the Welland Canal - the Keefer Mills (above) and George Keefer of Thorold, a direct decendant, unveiling a commemorative plaque (below).

To the south, the villages of Allanburg and Port Robinson are located at the two ends of the Deep Cut. Here is the scene of excitement during the mid-1820s, when labour gangs working on the Canal were faced with the most difficult task of excavation. Allanburg, where the Canal works were initiated, grew as a service centre with a lock providing motive power to its early industrial establishments. Port Robinson was where the First and Second Canals were locked down into the Welland River; a lock and nearby stores survive, and a former shipyard is marked by a plaque. Churches and residences of the mid-nineteenth century exist in both villages. Formerly more extensive and relatively more industrially active than today, Allanburg and Port Robinson were born, nurtured and sent into decline by the Canal enterprise.

Downtown Welland also grew with the Canal, being initiated where an aqueduct on the Feeder Canal crossed the Welland River, and with this channel and aqueduct becoming part of the First Canal in 1833. The urban core developed next to the Canal, primarily on its east bank. The importance of this position is demonstrated by the County Offices and Courthouse that were constructed next to the Welland River and the Canal in the mid-1850s.

The motto for the city of Welland, *"Where Rails and Waters Meet"*, reflects enthusiasm for a location at a mid-point of the Peninsula, a central position on the Canal, and a place where the Canal was crossed by a series of rail routes. Industry has taken advantage of these considerable locational opportunities, especially after cheap and abundant electricity was available from Niagara Falls. These industries, served with water from the Canal, follow the now-abandoned channel of the Fourth Canal.

Port Colborne began life when the Canal was extended to Gravelly Bay and opened for navigation on the direct through route between Lake Erie and Lake Ontario in 1833. Water then flowed south from the summit level at Welland to Port Colborne where harbour facilities developed. The port of entrance and its harbour have been changed by the Canal improvements of each successive Canal. Though buildings and roads have necessarily been removed, the banks have supported industries and services in association with the Canal from its inception to this day. Port Colborne is the most long-lived of Canal towns in immediate and continuing association with the Canal.

In these communities, street patterns have developed with the Canal. In St. Catharines and Thorold, the main streets (St. Paul and Front) are parallel to the Canal. In Welland and Port Colborne, where the Canal is crossed by major roads, developments along these routes are at right angles to the Canal. In Port Dalhousie, the main street (Lock Street) is focussed onto Lock 1 of the Second Canal, and an ably renewed street frontage faces the basin where ships formerly

Initiated by the aqueduct on the First Welland Canal, Welland grew astride the Canal. The scene is looking south from Main Street Bridge in 1958.

Public Archives Canada, c5958
George, Earl of Dalhousie

Public Archives Canada, c29891
William Hamilton Merritt

Public Archives Canada, c22381
Hon. John Beverley Robinson

Public Archives Canada, c10889
Sir John Colborne (shown as Lord Seaton)

Canal namesakes. Places along the Canal were named after patrons and sponsors of the First Welland Canal.

John Burtniak Collection

Port Colborne has grown with and been changed by the series of Welland Canals. These buildings on East Street, lining the Third Canal, were removed to make way for the present Canal.

entered the Canal system.

This pride of association with the Canal is recalled in place names. Friends and supporters of the initiating scheme are respected through naming Merritton after William Hamilton Merritt, its prime promoter; Port Colborne after Lieutenant-Governor Sir John Colborne; Port Dalhousie after Lord Dalhousie; Port Robinson after Chief Justice John Beverley Robinson, and Allanburg after the Hon. William Allan, a Director of the Welland Canal Company. St. Catharines, which preceded the Canal, by contrast is named after Catherine Hamilton, the wife of an early landowner in the community. The latest Canal name, Port Weller, recalls J.L. Weller, the Engineer in charge of construction operations from 1912 to 1917.

The Welland Canal, constructed as a slender ditch across the Peninsula in 1829, has become landscape of the highest order **and** a major sponsor of new landscape features. It serves a multitude of functions: it transfers ocean and lake vessels between Lake Erie and Lake Ontario; it is a tourist attraction because of its interesting features; it is a body of water tapped to supply a welter of industrial and municipal activities; it has created settlement and influenced their successive evolution; and it has provided a rich endowment of buildings and landscape characteristics that give the modern landscape much character. The Welland Canal is both a waterway of international importance and a significant agent of land development in the Niagara Peninsula.

1.9 A Modern Economic Appraisal

According to a survey conducted in 1979 for the Niagara Regional Chamber of Commerce, in St. Catharines alone about 5,500 local residents drew more than $118,955,000 in wages directly related to the marine industry. Local spending by shipping lines and other branches of the industry added at least another $57,600,000. As there are approximately 3,400 local residents for whom the ships provided employment, wages of more than $75,550,000 were brought into the local economy.

The largest single employer continues to be Port Weller Dry Docks, with about 700 em-ployees and an annual payroll of $12,000,000, while the St. Lawrence Seaway Authority provides more than 650 jobs in the operation of the Welland Canal with a payroll estimated at $12,700,000.

Port Weller Dry Docks

Port Weller Dry Docks

Ship repair, maintenance and construction are undertaken at Port Weller Dry Docks, St. Catharines.

The operation of the Canal, movement of cargo, and construction and repair of ships, remain the dominant part of the industry's effects on Niagara. Numerous smaller companies depend on ships and shipping for their existence. These suppliers and contractors provide services essential to the maintenance and operation of the Canadian vessels which regularly use the Welland Canal. These ships spend an average of $251,000 each year in the Niagara area for supplies and services—a total of $37,650,000, not including crew payrolls and fuel purchases. These expenditures create more jobs as suppliers and contractors go to their suppliers and sub-contractors for a direct spinoff of more than $58,700,000.

In addition to the local residents who man the ships, their co-workers who make their homes elsewhere in the winter months are estimated to spend close to $3,000,000 in area stores and commercial outlets during their hours ashore.

Other areas which benefit from the day-to-day operations are taxi services which move crew members and Great Lakes pilots to and from the ships. Hotels draw business from company and supplier representatives; one company alone estimated its visitors accounted for the rental of 500 hotel rooms, without even considering the side effect on the food trade.

Not included are retail outlets and contractors with no apparent connection with the marine industry—the construction and electrical contractors who work each winter along the Welland Canal, rehabilitating facilities, and completing repairs which cannot be undertaken by the St. Lawrence Seaway Authority's own work force.

There are appliance stores, such as the one which sold 100 colour television sets in one year

to ships of the Canadian fleets, which are also big purchasers of washing machines and dryers. These ships also need drapery, carpeting and paint. One shipping line buys all its paint needs from one local firm.

Most marine shipping companies have offices along the Canal and numerous other companies have located close by the Canal, supplying and servicing the ships from a local base. This is highly visible in the Cushman Road area of St. Catharines with its mix of service outlets and offices, and at Port Colborne. Non-Canadian fleet operations also make a *"considerable contribution"* to the economy of the Welland Canal area.

In Port Colborne, a study of 1980 has indicated that nine businesses and industries, employing 324 persons with a payroll of $8.0 million, derived their livelihood directly from the Canal as ship suppliers, repairs and bunkering;

Fred A. Addis

Ships load stone for export to U.S. ports at Port Colborne.

Fred A. Addis

The break-up of outmoded vessels by Marine Salvage Company Limited on the abandoned Third Canal at Port Colborne.

six companies employing 413 persons and a payroll of $9.85 million, are described as **"captive to the Seaway"**, including flour millers, grain terminals, stone quarries and coal docks; and two companies, with 150 employees and a payroll of $4.0 million, use its facilities in the conduct of business. This is a total of 837 jobs and a payroll of $21.8 million, quite apart from further service and commercial activities. The Canal is of exceptional importance to the Niagara Peninsula—visually, historically, for its trade and contribution to the pattern of settlement, and in terms of its long-term economic vitality and contributions.

St. Lawrence Seaway Authority

The St. Lawrence Seaway Authority is a major employer in the Niagara Peninsula. Malcolm S. Campbell, Vice President Western Region, is shown presenting a 25-year service award to Leo Clutterbuck, a rigger.

46

II
Places of Interest along the Canal

2.1 Canal Access and Its Major Features

Access to the Canal is from all east-west roads that cross its line. Roads along the **west bank** generally offer the best viewing locations. Remember always that this is a *fully-operating waterway managed and controlled by the St. Lawrence Seaway Authority. Under no circumstances should any action be taken which interferes with the movement of ships. Visitors are privileged witnesses of the scene, and must obey the warning signs that exist. There is no public right of entry to many of the places that are mentioned. The Canal waters are also deep and dangerous. Swimming, boating and fishing are not allowed on waters in use for navigation.*

Features along the Canal such as its bridges are numbered from north to south. This may be confusing to some because the flow of water is from south to north. Upbound ships *"ascend"* the Canal from Port Weller on Lake Ontario to Port Colborne on Lake Erie; downbound ships *"descend"* the Canal.

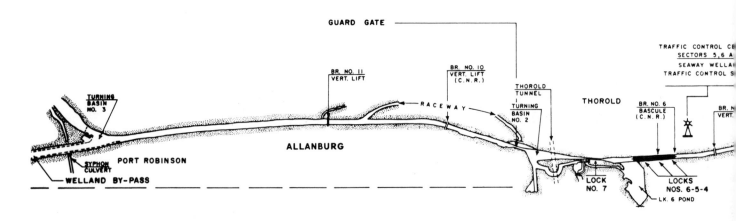

General Plan : Welland

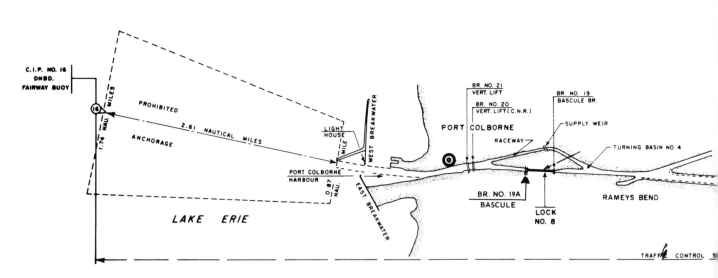

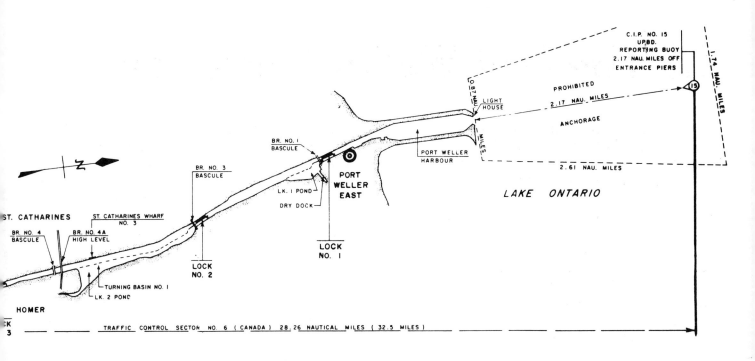

C.I.P. NO. 15
UP.BD.
REPORTING BUOY
2.17 NAU. MILES OFF
ENTRANCE PIERS

PROHIBITED

2.17 NAU. MILES

ANCHORAGE

2.61 NAU. MILES

1.74 NAU. MILES

LIGHT HOUSE

0.87 NAU.

MILES

BR. NO. 1
BASCULE

PORT WELLER HARBOUR

LAKE ONTARIO

PORT WELLER EAST

LK. 1 POND

DRY DOCK

LOCK NO. 1

BR. NO. 3
BASCULE

ST. CATHARINES

ST. CATHARINES WHARF NO. 3

BR. NO. 4
BASCULE

BR. NO. 4A
HIGH LEVEL

TURNING BASIN NO. 1

LK. 2 POND

LOCK NO. 2

HOMER

CK 3

TRAFFIC CONTROL SECTOR NO. 6 (CANADA) 28.26 NAUTICAL MILES (32.5 MILES)

anal

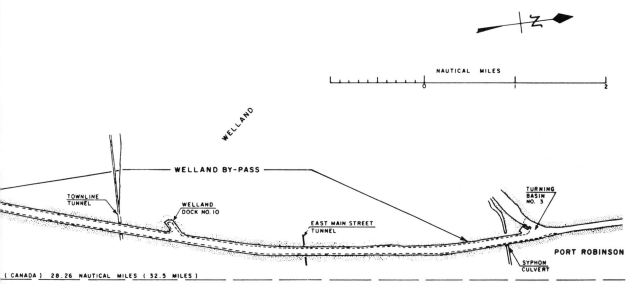

NAUTICAL MILES

0   1   2

WELLAND

WELLAND BY-PASS

TOWNLINE
TUNNEL

WELLAND
DOCK NO. 10

EAST MAIN STREET
TUNNEL

TURNING
BASIN
NO. 3

PORT ROBINSON

SYPHON
CULVERT

(CANADA) 28.26 NAUTICAL MILES (32.5 MILES)

Amended from The Seaway Handbook

2.2 The Port Weller Entrance

Two pincer-shaped breakwaters extend the Welland Canal for 2.25 km (1.4 miles) into Lake Ontario. The materials that compose these breakwaters were excavated from the channel to the south including the site of the flight locks, and were deposited in the Lake from a construction railway. The breakwaters enclose Port Weller Harbour. The entrance is narrow at 122 m (400 feet) wide. The central channel through the Harbour, excavated to bedrock in the Lake bottom, is aligned on a direct compass bearing of 180° (south). A lighthouse, visible from across the Lake, has been erected on the west side, its fog horn sounds for two seconds, and is then silent for eight. As the currents of Lake Ontario are from west to east along the lakeshore, some infilling of the Lake by deposition is taking place in the bay east of the breakwaters.

Ships may be anchored in the designated anchorage in Lake Ontario awaiting entry to Port Weller Harbour and passage through the Canal. They are berthed on either side of the Harbour during the closed season and on the western side when waiting entry to Lock 1 during the navigation season. A small dock on the east side may house pilot vessels, tugs or other small craft. North of the pleasure craft dock, the St. Lawrence Seaway Authority moors its floating equipment. The breakwaters have been landscaped. Access exists to both banks, but is superior on the west side where informal picnic areas exist between Lake Ontario and Port Weller Harbour. Travelling south, the line of the original shore line is clearly visible by the rise of slope up the former bluffs.

John N Jackson

The Port Weller entrance to the Canal showing the breakwaters, Lock 1, Bridge 1, and the weir that regulates the flow of water.

John N. Jackson

Ships anchored in Lake Ontario await passage through the Canal.

Lock 1 (a single lock), Bridge 1 (a single leaf rolling-lift bridge that carries both a highway and the *Canadian National* tracks of the former *Niagara, St. Catharines and Toronto Electric Railway)*, and the regulating waste weir water levels on the upper reach, are followed by the Port Weller Dry Docks with dry docks and fitting out berths next to the Canal on the east bank. This dock site, a former pondage area for Lock 1 and gate yard for repairing and maintaining seaway floating equipment, is now occupied by one of the foremost Canadian ship building and ship repairing yards on the Great Lakes. Port Weller Dry Docks is successor to other shipyards which have played an important role in the marine industrial fabric of St. Catharines (including Port Dalhousie) since the first Welland Canal was built early in the nineteenth century. Since its beginning in 1946, the yard has built a variety of ships including self-unloading bulk carriers, tankers, ice breakers and ice strengthened ships.

Port Weller Dry Docks

Shipbuilding is an important activity along the Canal. Port Weller Dry Docks at the northern entrance constructs vessels for Great Lakes and Ocean service.

2.3 The Northern Length

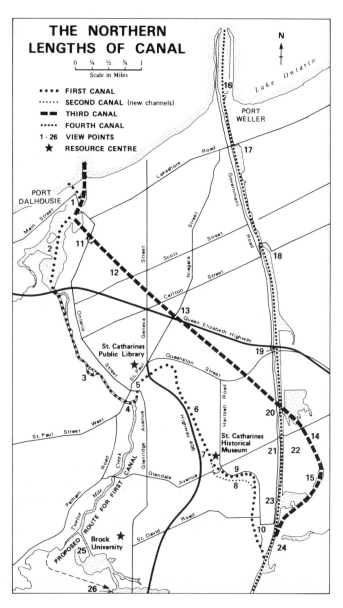

THE NORTHERN LENGTHS OF CANAL

0   ¼   ½   ¾   1
Scale in Miles

•••• FIRST CANAL
•••••• SECOND CANAL (new channels)
▬ ▬ THIRD CANAL
••••• FOURTH CANAL
1 - 26 VIEW POINTS
★ RESOURCE CENTRE

1. Port Dalhousie. A canal-oriented community at the entrance to the First, Second and Third Canals.
2. Martindale Pond. An artificial lake created by the dam at Port Dalhousie. Home of the Henley Rowing Regatta.
3. Welland Vale. Second Canal lock. Water-power from the First and Second Canals harnessed for industrial purposes.
4. Meeting point of the Canal valley with Twelve Mile Creek. Industry formerly on the right bank; Schickluna shipyards on left bank.
5. The Central Business District of St. Catharines, Industrial growth and urban evolution in close association with the First and Second Canals, and their hydraulic raceways. Note St. Paul Street, front and rear on the south side, as the commercial front door to the City from the Canal Valley.
6. Oakdale. Locks of the Second Canal. Note diminishing depth of the Canal valley to the south.
7. Main line rail tracks here crossed the Second Canal which, with water power, made Merritton into a place of industrial advantage.
8. Bradley Street. Second Canal locks here climb the Escarpment.
9. Thorold-Merritton industrial strip along the First and Second Canals.
10. Thorold. A canal-oriented community astride the First and Second Welland Canals.
11. Third Canal Locks.
12. Third Canal infilled, but reflected in street alignments.
13. Third Canal corridor crossed by Queen Elizabeth Way.
14. Flight Locks of the Third Canal.
15. Railway tunnel under the Third Canal.
16. Port Weller. Artificial harbour and entry point to the Fourth Canal.
17. Port Weller Dry Docks.
18. Fourth Canal, Lock 2. Canal raised above neighbouring terrain.
19. The Garden City Skyway, and the former village of Homer.
20. Fourth Canal, Lock 3. Official viewing area. Tourist information.
21. St. Lawrence Seaway Authority: Regional Offices and Control Centre.
22. General Motors plant using industrial water from the Fourth Canal.
23. Double set of Flight Locks, crossing the Escarpment.
24. Divergent water systems serving the Third and Fourth Canal systems.
25. DeCew Generating Station, supplied with water from the Fourth Canal at Allanburg.
26. DeCew Falls. The intended route of the First Canal to Twelve Mile Creek.

The northern length of the Canal, between the Escarpment and Lake Ontario, crosses the famed Niagara Fruit Belt, important through its soil and climatic characteristics for the production of grapes, peaches and cherries. Ships can indeed be photographed with either blossoms or a harvest of fruit in the foreground. The Canal along its northern length also provides the generalized physical divide, though not the administrative boundary, between the urban characteristics of the City of St. Catharines to the west and the Fruit Belt east to the Niagara River.

Department of Geography, Brock University

The slope of the Ontario Plain is overcome by three separated lift locks, as the canal rises towards the Escarpment (Locks 1, 2 and 3). Bridge 3 on Carlton Street in St. Catharines is combined with Lock 2, its attendant pondage, and a regulating weir on the east bank. The Queen Elizabeth Way and the Garden City Skyway follow, together with the historic Queenston to St. Catharines road that follows a former shoreline of Lake Ontario. This road is famous both as a major Indian route (the Iroquois Trail), and as a pioneer route of entry for United Empire Loyalists entering Upper Canada after the American Revolution. It is the road on which St. Catharines grew, first as a rural service centre and then as an industrial city in conjunction with the Canal.

Where the Canal crosses this road (old Highway 8, now Highway 81) was the Village of Homer, now part of St. Catharines. Its interest, apart from the unusual classical name (Virgil is nearby), is that the village pre-dates the Canal. It grew as an independent centre, but the nucleus was destroyed when the Fourth Canal was constructed and by the Garden City Skyway and its approaching ramps. Remnants, including buildings and a cemetery, survive on either side of Bridge 4, a double leaf, rolling-lift bridge with two highway lanes and two sidewalks. On the west bank, a restaurant overlooks the Canal; it has been designed with a dining lounge that provides panoramic views of passing ships. To the north are mooring posts and the St. Catharines Wharf, with nearby oil tanks and a turning basin for vessels up to 107 metres (350 feet) in length.

St. Lawrence Seaway Authority

Bridge crossings over the northern length of Canal.

53

To the south, Lock 3 provides a prime viewing area of the Canal. An adjacent park contains a no charge, raised observation platform for visitors to watch ships pass through the lock, information and display buildings, various commemorative plaques, parking space for cars and coaches, picnic space in landscaped surroundings, a refreshment booth, and public washrooms. A unique marine sign-post provides the sailing distance to various world ports, including 1,447 km (899 miles) to Chicago in the United States and 5,763 km (3,579 miles) to London, England—an instructive reminder both of the Canal's international role, and its distance from the sea in the North American interior.

Apart from ship watching, the former presence of the Third Canal should be noted. The Fourth Canal crossed the Third Canal at the south end of Lock 3. To the northwest the former channel to Port Dalhousie has been infilled, but its route can be gleaned from streets that run across the regular-shaped pattern of survey grid streets in St. Catharines. To the southeast, the channel with its flow of water and extant locks provides pondage for the modern Canal. These locks provide an interesting comparison to their modern counterparts. They are located east of the Canal behind the General Motors Plant. For view are the fine lock sequences as the Third Canal appoached the Escarpment, and many of the accompanying sluices and ponds. The area contains an informal recreational environment, with trails approaching the several locks for their close inspection. ***Beware of the flowing water, which is deep and subject to sudden changes of level.***

St. Lawrence Seaway Authority

The viewer observation platform at Lock 3, a popular place to view the parade of passing ships.

Lock 3 and its waste weir on the modern Canal were completed in 1926, but only after a series of landslides caused construction difficulties. Lock construction has been facilitated by the geological structure of the Peninsula. The base rocks of alternating limestones, shales and sandstone dip slightly south, which means that a sequence of strata are crossed by the Canal. When the Fourth Canal was constructed, it proved possible to site all its major works on sound bedrock. The swing of the road around Lock 3 is the route of the construction railway for the Fourth Canal where it crossed the Third Canal.

John Burtniak Collection

The Mountain Locks: The Third Canal crossing the Niagara Escarpment (above), and what survives to-day (below).

John N. Jackson

Where east meets west! The Canal signpost at Lock 3.

John N. Jackson

2.4 Canal History in St. Catharines

At Lock 3, there is a directional sign to the St. Catharines Historical Museum, 3.2 km (two miles) west of the Canal in Merritton at 343 Merritt Street. Built in 1874 from local stone and used as the Merritton Municipal Building until this community was incorporated into St. Catharines against strong citizen objections, it houses displays, maps and papers pertinent to the sequence of Canal developments. The Reference Collection in the St. Catharines Public Library at 54 Church Street in downtown also has a focus of attention on the history of the City and its Canals, as has Brock University. There is an extensive collection of Canal related materials in the University Library, and maps, charts and air photographs may be viewed in the University Map Library in the Department of Geography.

St. Catharines is endowed with many significant Canal features through its long term associations with the ongoing sequence of Canals. These features are located primarily at Port Dalhousie, in and close to the downtown area, and along the Canal valley to Merritton and the Thorold boundary. A Merrittrail, a 22.5 km (14 mile) bicycle and walking trail constructed through the initiative of the Welland Canals Preservation Association with financial assistance from many local industries and the several levels of government, winds it way along the Second Canal and interlinks its many features as a con-

tinuity. Access is at the many points where roads in the city cross the Second Canal.

Port Dalhousie, the harbour on Lake Ontario for the first three Canals, retains important remnants from these hectic years. Its surviving features include renovated buildings which serviced the Canal and the men who worked its ships, Lock Street with its focus on Lock 1 of the Second Canal, Martindale Pond where the Henley Rowing Regatta is now staged, restored buildings of the Muir Dry Dock, twin piers built in 1851 with two lighthouses (one large, one small), Lock 1 and weir structures of the Third Canal, an 1850 jail, and the Lakeside recreational park with a nineteenth century carousel.

Downtown St. Catharines is also a creature of the Canal. It grew from a village to an industrial town and gained strength as a city from the transportation, water power and industrial advantages of the First and Second Canals. When the Third Canal by-passed this centre, the Second Canal remained in use to service industrial premises along its route. Most of the buildings and sites developed before the nineteenth century have some Canal relevance.

These historic landmarks include the home of William Hamilton Merritt (now the CKTB radio station) on the bank of the Canal near its junction with Twelve Mile Creek, the first high-level fixed bridge that crossed the Canal (Burgoyne Bridge), the site of the famous Shickluna Ship-

J.D. Barnes Limited, Toronto, from University Map Library, Department of Geography, Brock University.

Port Dalhousie Canal and village, in 1974.

John N. Jackson

Lock 1, Third Canal, with gates intact at 1966.

John N. Jackson

Tasteful renewal of a marine hardware and grocery store that served vessels on the Canal.

John N. Jackson

Martindale Pond, home of the Henley Rowing Regatta.

John Burtniak Collection

The dam constructed across the Twelve Mile Creek for the Second Welland Canal provided water power and encouraged industrial development. Only the mill on the right survives.

John N. Jackson

Lock tenders hut next to the Third Canal, indicating the quality of Canal architecture.

Scenes at Port Dalhousie.

58

H. Brosius, 1875

John N. Jackson

John Burtniak Collection

The townscape of St. Catharines owes a considerable debt to the Canals that passed its front doorstep. St. Paul Street, a notable street frontage, follows a curving alignment above the Canal valley.

yard below this bridge which produced over 200 ships for service on the Canal in the mid-nineteenth century, and nearby industrial premises on the opposite bank such as the Taylor and Bate's Brewery and Lincoln Foundry—now removed and replaced by a four-lane, provincial road (Highway 406) in the Canal Valley. The Court House of the now defunct Lincoln County exemplifies the transfer of legal and administrative activities from Niagara-on-the-Lake to the new centre of activity, and names such as Race and Head Streets provide the necessary reminder that the industrial base of St. Catharines emerged in conjunction with hydraulic raceways fed upstream from the Canal along its northern bank.

Merriton, named after William Hamilton Merritt who founded the Canal, grew in close association with the first two Canals. The flight of six locks, where the second Canal crossed the Escarpment, may be viewed from Bradley Street. The locks are constructed of resistant dolomitic limestone brought to the site from the Niagara Escarpment. They are aligned along a sloping part of the hillside below the Escarpment, parallel to the scarp face, and on a base of glacial materials deposited during the Ice Age. Facing certain locks are the semi-detached homes of locktenders; these have considerable character because of age and because they are constructed of local red Grimsby sandstone from the Escarpment. The blackened tower and structure of a rubber mill (a previous cotton factory), and the site of the Riordan paper mill (the first paper and sulphide mill in Canada), show how the Canal provides the reminder of a waterway that attracted industry to its banks.

John N. Jackson

Ontario Archives ST406, from
St. Catharines Historical Museum

The Second Canal crossing the Escarpment at Bradley Street, Merritton.

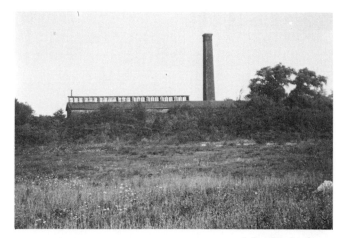

Industrial buildings next to the Second Canal at Merritton, rubber mill (left) and the Riordan paper mill (right).

2.5 The Canal Crosses the Escarpment

This length, defined as from Bridge 5 (Glenridge Avenue in St. Catharines) past the Flight Locks to Lock 7 (the last of the lift locks) is the most memorable part of the Canal system. Locks 4, 5 and 6 (the twin flight locks in Thorold) permit the simultaneous locking of ships in both directions. Their viewing areas offer a favoured locality from which the Canal, the detail of its passing ships, and the extensive vista north over the Fruit Belt to Lake Ontario (with Toronto visible on a clear day) may be studied.

Bridge 5, a vertical lift bridge not associated with a lock, is the only one of its type north of the Escarpment face. Immediately to the south is the interesting juxtaposition of two important building complexes that reflect the diverse theme of the Welland Canal: the Seaway offices and General Motors. The Western Region Offices of the St. Lawrence Seaway Authority at 508 Glendale Avenue contain the traffic control centre for ships in and approaching the Welland Canal, administrative, engineering, and maintenance offices. Here is the hub of the Canal system, which began as an office in the private residence of William Hamilton Merritt when the Welland Canal Company was first initiated. Offices were constructed and expanded next to the Canal in downtown St. Catharines (now demolished) and, with the Seaway commitment, these facilities were moved to their present site close to the Fourth Canal.

John N. Jackson

General Motors (above), the major employer of the Niagara Peninsula, faces the Western Region Offices of the St. Lawrence Seaway Authority (below) across the Canal at Glendale Avenue, St. Catharines.

St. Lawrence Seaway Authority

On the east bank, a General Motors plant (one of three in St. Catharines) sustains the principal centre of employment in both St. Catharines and the Niagara Region. It was intended in the 1940s that the production of engine and other automotive parts would be exported by water to Oshawa for assembly into completed vehicles. An intended wharf on the Canal, a water supply from the Canal for its industrial processes, the location of the initiating enterprise in downtown St. Catharines on St. Paul Street backed by a hydraulic raceway, and a new plant on Ontario Street next to the Second Canal, together furnish a series of ongoing associations between this industrial activity and the Canal system. As other buggy and early automobile plants had canal-oriented sites (the REO plant, which produced the first automobile to cross Canada was located at the southern end of Geneva Street), it is doubtful if the major economic base of manufacturing automotive parts would have risen in St. Catharines without the Canal.

A power house is located next to Lock 4 at the foot of the Flight Locks on the west bank. This structure generates power for the operation of the Canal, including its locks, bridges and illumination. The rounded and pointed vertical feature that looks rather like a rocket is a surge tank. The head of water is drawn to the turbines from above Lock 7, providing a fall of 56.69 m (186 feet). The Seaway is self-sufficient and independent from the Ontario grid for its hydro-electric requirements.

Bridge 6, a rolling lift bridge with two separated spans, carries the double track of the main line **Canadian National** railway across the Canal. When trains are approaching the Canal, the spans cannot be lifted. As the tracks are also

here climbing the Niagara Escarpment, this is a strategic point where major Canadian land and water communications meet. It was the first of such crossings in the Peninsula, originating in 1853 when the **Great Western** Railway (then **Grand Trunk,** now **Canadian National**) crossed the Second Canal at Merritton en route to the Suspension Bridge across the Niagara Gorge and U.S. connections. The north-south Welland Railway was soon added, following the length of the Canal on its east bank from Port Colborne to Port Dalhousie. Merritton grew with a threefold set of locational advantages: waterpower from the Canal, shipping services and rail access. History and geography in explanation of the Canal scene are closely intertwined in the Welland situation.

When the Third Canal was aligned along a new route in the 1880s, its channel had necessarily to be crossed by the pre-existing railway system. The rail track was rerouted in a circular route to the south and taken under the Third Canal by a tunnel. This may be viewed about one quarter of a mile south of the **Canadian National** rail bridge on the road taken to view the Escarpment locks of the Third Canal. Here the road bends slightly to the left (east), with a white guard rail on the right side of the road. The tunnel entrance is below, on the right of the road, for those who have the agility to scramble down the steep embankment. Trees carry the white blaze of the Bruce Trail Association (a long distance hiking trail from Queenston Heights to Tobermory), but only the foolhardy will enter the tunnel as it leaks and the ground is exceptionally muddy. The tunnel entrance is dignified with magnificent stonework that might be compared with the quality workmanship of the Second and Third Canal locks.

(Inset) Robin Brown, STELCO

St. Catharines Historical Museum

The Grand Trunk Railway tunnel under the Third Canal south of Glendale Avenue, St. Catharines, ca. 1887, with inset showing the quality of the stonework.

The Flight Locks, a triple series of double locks, are world famous.

Locks 4, 5 and 6, the so-called Flight Locks because no Canal reach separates them, are like three giant steps in an enormous flight of stairs. This exceptionally attractive length of Canal may be approached either north along Canal Road in Thorold, or south from Glendale Avenue onto Government Road in St. Catharines. Limited visitor viewing space is available on the west bank at the top of Locks 5 and 6, with the latter providing an extensive panoramic view north along the Canal to the Garden City Skyway. Limited parking space is available next to Locks 4 and 5, but inside the wire fences is private property owned and operated by the Seaway Authority. *The lock area is hazardous and must not be entered by the public. Visitors are not allowed into the lock precincts. We are privileged to view the scene. Please do not abuse this freedom.*

The flight provides a total lift of 42.6 m (139.5 feet), the maximum dimensions of the locks are 261.81 m (859 feet) long, 24.38 m (80 feet) wide with 9.14 m (30 feet) of water over the gate sills. For safety reasons, the maximum size of vessel permitted to transit the Seaway must not exceed 222.5 m (730 feet) overall, 23.16 m (76 feet) extreme breadth, or draw more than 7.92 m (26 feet) fresh water draft. No vessel less than 6.10 m (20 feet) in overall length, or 907.18 kg (1 ton) in weight, may use the Canal.

The Flight Locks were the last of the eight locks to be constructed. Completed in 1932 they were, and continue to be, a great engineering feat. Their height is well illustrated by the height of the concrete wall at the north end of Lock 5; this, from the coping of Lock 5 to the bottom of Lock 4, amounts to 39.8 m (130.8 feet). By way

of contrast the Horseshoe Falls at Niagara Falls are 53.6 m (176 feet) high.

Their significance might also be stressed by noting that Locks 4, 5 and 6 have a length of almost 1,250 m (4,100 feet). Their rise of 42.52 m (139.5 feet) may be compared with a lift of 25.91 m (85 feet) for the three locks at Gatun on the Panama Canal. The Welland Canal, when constructed, and to this day, involves engineering works which place it in the front rank of world canals.

The water supply culverts are continuous, so that the water from one lock discharges directly into the one below. The intakes for the Flight Locks are placed in an isolated pondage area east of the reach between Locks 6 and 7. The culverts are 3.7 m (12 feet) wide by 5.0 m (16.5 feet) high. There are four culverts, one in each of the east and west walls, and one on each side of the concrete centre wall separating the east and west lock chambers. The water is controlled at each lock by discharge valves. For emphasis is that the locks are filled and emptied through small passages 0.9 m (3 feet) wide by 1.2 m (4 feet) high at the **bottom** of the lock walls. These passages are connected to the large water supply culverts which run lengthwise along the lock. The locks are filled neither through the gates, nor through tanks in the central lock wall.

The operating mitre gates are built entirely of steel. They are 14.63 m (48 feet) long, 1.5 m (5 feet) wide. The lower gates are 25 m (82 feet) high and each leaf weighs 497,862.98 kg (490 tons); the upper gates are 10.8 m (35.5 feet) high and each leaf weighs 193 tonnes. Their hanging was a task of exceptional difficulty, unfortunately resulting in the most serious accident of the construction works for the whole length of the Canal. A locomotive crane on the lock walls toppled into the lock chamber, upsetting a partially erected service gate, killing 12 persons.

As it would be a serious matter if a gate were carried away by a vessel, a not uncommon occurrence on the Third Canal, *"ship arresters"* have been provided to protect the gates. These arresters consist of 8.89 cm (3.5 inch) diameter steel rope stretched across the lock, being carried on a light structural steel arm which raises or lowers the cable across the lock. The tension on these cables is designed to stop a vessel before it strikes the gates.

The gates, valves and ship arresters are all operated electrically by remote control from control rooms located at the north ends of Locks 4, 5 and 6, and one at the south end of Lock 6. All equipment is electrically inter-locked to help

Hugh J. Gayler

The convergence of major modes of transportation to cross the Niagara Escarpment.

John N. Jackson

The scene north from the Flight Locks, with ship arrester boom and cable to protect the gates in the foreground.

prevent accidents or incidents from human error.

Since the Flight Locks are twinned to allow the simultaneous two-way passage of ships, up-bound vessels normally transit the west side and downbound vessels normally transit the east side. The dumping time for each lock is approximately 11 minutes. the transit time for a vessel through the Flight Locks is about 1.5 hours, with transit through the entire Canal taking approximately 12 hours.

The Flight Locks were constructed next to the built-up area of Thorold, where the central business district had developed around the routes of the First and Second Canals. Much evidence remains of these routes. The Third Canal by-passed Thorold and, when the Fourth Canal was constructed, buildings, a water supply reservoir and railway track had each to be moved and re-located so that road, rail and Canal now parallel each other to surmount the Escarpment at the same point. The Flight Locks have brought world distinction to the City of Thorold where, as described in many brochures, *"the ships of all nations climb the mountain."*

To the south, Lock 7 (a single lock) is the last lift lock in the passage of the Canal over the Escarpment. Ships are often moored in this vicinity, and may be viewed close by when passing through the lock. The Fourth Canal here begins its route north direct to Lake Ontario, departing from the channel of the Third Canal which may be viewed on the east bank together with the horizontal rock formations of the Niagara Escarpment. A considerable water complex, much changed through time, includes supply and regulating weirs, together with large storage ponds on streams backed up on the east side of the Canal, and a turning basin for vessels up to 183 m (600 feet) long between Lock 7 and its upstream guard gate.

It is a complex environment with many Canal, industrial and urban-related features that grade west into a prime residential area of Thorold. The Lock 7 motel and restaurant on Chapel Street is worthy of note: it is the only such facility in immediate association with the Canal on its length through the Peninsula; its rooms and balconies overlook the Canal, providing a convenient viewing platform of passing ships and the locks.

2.6 Thorold

Downtown Thorold grew next to the First and Second Canals, but was divested of the waterway when the Third Canal by-passed the town. The water power and trading advantages of the Canal are reflected in the Welland Mills of 1846 that produced up to 500 barrels of flour a day, and by the gracious three storey Maplehurst mansion overlooking the Canal. This house was built by John Keefer, a former President of the Welland Canal Company. The old fire hall next to the Canal is another distinctive building. The Canal, now infilled and in part used for the provision of public open space, is also lined with industrial premises such as paper mills that use water from the Canal. Front Street, the main commercial street, parallels the former Second Canal; its location and nineteenth century architecture recall the creative role of the Canal as the founder of new settlements.

The eastern end of the Thorold Tunnel contains rock exposures depicting the geological history of the Escarpment. The terrain is less fertile and bedrock lies closer to the surface than on the Ontario Plain. We have left the Fruit Belt, for an area with more mixed farming. Next to the Canal at the eastern end of the tunnel are private industrial docks and facilities for the bulk outdoor storage of coal, building supplies, coke and carbon products.

The Canal, throughout history and today, has always been a strong force for the attraction of industry. This fact is well exemplified by the Ontario Paper Company, located next to the Canal south of Lock 7 on the east bank. This site, with major docking facilities, provides a neat essay for the student of industrial location. It originated in

John N. Jackson

The Welland Mills, a major industrial survival, next to the Second Canal in Thorold.

John N. Jackson

A ship passes over the Thorold tunnel with its architecturally-designed entrance.

Thorold in the 1930's, with the Second Canal (foreground) still intact as a water body and the Fourth Canal bounding the town.

Picturesque Canada, 1882

The pride of historical association in Thorold, the same scene separated by a century of time.

John N Jackson

1910-1911 on the Third Canal, because pulpwood could be imported by Canal, and paper could be shipped by water easily to Chicago. The area was served by several railroads. It was not far from the coal mines of Pennsylvania and Ohio, with transport again being feasible by water, and it was near the settled community of Thorold, with an abundance of cheap hydroelectric power being available from the Ontario Power Company at Niagara Falls. The stamp of industrial opportunities was placed on Thorold by the fortuitous presence of the Canal.

This modern industrial importance of the Canal is soon appreciated. The scene, though not necessarily visually attractive, is nevertheless of great economic significance for Thorold and the Niagara Region. If the Canal is followed along its east bank from Thorold to Allanburg (the west bank here carries a succession of former channels), two major industrial landscapes can be viewed south of Ontario Paper. Beaver Wood Fibre (boxboard, plasterboard and paper) and Hayes Dana (automotive parts) are close to the Canal, and both are served by rail facilities. It is *"proceed at your own risk"* next to the Canal, but the reward is that you are immediately next to the Canal and its shipping activity. Informal parking and picnic space exists on banks that have been pleasantly landscaped with lines of trees. Functionally, the trees provide a windbreak for passing ships.

2.7 Allanburg and Port Robinson

The foundation of the Canal's history is recognized at Allanburg. A cairn in a park at the west end of Bridge 11 commemorates the formal opening of construction works in 1824. Two features may be observed nearby: the hydro and water supply cuts that feed the lake complex at DeCew Falls, and the so-called *"Deep Cut"* to the south. The Deep Cut, where excavation in the mid 1820s caused so much difficulty through landslides, is also the only length of Canal where each successor Canal has followed the same alignment. The Cut, successively widened and deepened, passes through a low ridge that rises to some 15.25 m (50 feet) above the Canal. Village buildings, including old frame houses that bear evidence of being former stores, are of more than passing interest.

Having lost its highway bridge across the Canal through accidental demolition by an errant ship in 1974, Port Robinson has the invidious distinction of being amputated into an eastern and a western village by the Canal. A six

Picturesque Canada, 1882

Francis J. Petrie Collection, 1978
Allanburg developed at the northern end of the Deep Cut. The cairn, where construction works commenced in 1824, is at the near side of the bridge.

John N. Jackson
The Deep Cut, south of Allanburg, yesterday and to-day.

passenger, no cargo ferry, the only such vessel on the Canal, plies seasonally between the two banks. Local residents wishing to cross the Canal by car now must travel via Allanburg or Welland.

Port Robinson grew where the First and Second Canals were locked down into the Welland River. A company of Black soldiers were stationed here to keep law and order among

John N. Jackson

The Canal By-Pass at Welland required the re-routing of railways and the Welland River. A new bridge here spans the new river at Port Robinson.

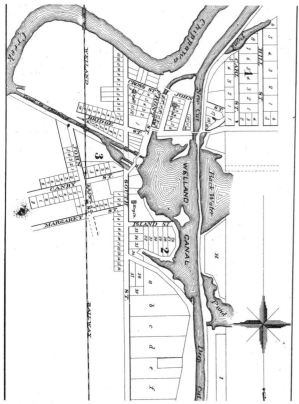

H. R. Page, Historical Atlas, 1876

The layout of Port Robinson remains clearly recognizable in the present day village.

workers on the Second Canal. A lock of the Second Canal, nearby stores, the site of a shipyard, angles of bend in the former main street across the Canal, street names, and several residential, commercial and church buildings provide important reminders of this formative past. The River remains, though as a dead-end channel after the construction of the By-Pass channel and a new length of River to the south. The contrasting scales of the By-Pass as the latest major canal project and the now abandoned channel of the Fourth Canal are best perceived from the east bank at Port Robinson. The syphon culvert which takes the Welland River under the By-Pass, and the new channel for the River might also be studied. The syphon has four tubes that can take 340 m³ (12,000 cubic feet of water) per second.

2.8 Welland and the By-Pass Channel

The winding stretch of the Fourth Canal through the City of Welland interfered heavily with road traffic when the lift bridges were raised and a railroad swing bridge, constructed with a central pier in mid-channel, restricted ship sizes and provided a major navigational hazard. The By-Pass, announced in 1965 and completed in 1973, involved no locks, but a considerable number of major changes were introduced to the Welland area. The By-Pass lies to the east of the developed area, but the impact was considerable over an extensive regional area.

The first three Canals, because of their shallower depth, were taken over the Welland River in central Welland by aqueduct. Greater depth in the Fourth Canal required that the River be taken under the Canal by an inverted syphon. When the Welland By-Pass was constructed, a second syphon took the Welland River under the new channel at Port Robinson. As noted, the River was diverted south with the former chan-

John N. Jackson

John N. Jackson

A syphon culvert takes the Welland River under the abandoned Fourth Canal (above), and then the By-Pass Channel (below).

St. Lawrence Seaway Authority

Not the Suez Canal but the Welland Canal By-Pass at Welland.

75

nel surviving as an isolated arm. There can be few, if any, rivers in the world that receive this incredible treatment of being taken twice under the same navigable waterway.

Water flow through the abandoned channel has been disrupted by the western approach to the Townline railway tunnel, and is no longer continuous. The Southern Reach (from the junction of the new and abandoned channels at Ramey's Bend to the railway cutting) is open to the new channel, but there is no through flow of water because an earthen coffer dam has been placed across the Channel. Flow in the Northern Reach has been retained, but it is a *"back-flow"* or reversal situation which is now south from Port Robinson towards Welland. Holes were drilled in the syphon to permit Canal water to flow into the Welland River, where it is used for dilution purposes and to serve the Welland waterworks. Water in the Northern Reach does not flow into the Central Reach (the length between the railway cutting and Main Street), and the Central Reach like the Southern Reach has no flow of water. The northern end of the abandoned channel is used as a turning basin for vessels 223 m (730 feet) in length, a facility that in 1981 promoted a zoning of land to permit shipbuilding at this location.

The abandoned channel, deemed suitable for a four-lane highway by the provincial and regional highway departments, has been saved for recreational purposes by staunch public protest. Designated a recreational waterway, the various reaches are in the process of vital transformation to a sequence of designed open spaces. Various power boat, rowing, canoeing and water skiing events now take place during the summer months. Boat ramps have been provided, as

have opportunities for swimming, hiking and picnicking along the west side of the former Canal banks.

Along the By-Pass, material excavated for the channel was placed on both banks in contoured

Department of Geography, Brock University

Local History Collection, Welland Public Library

The abandoned channel of the Fourth Canal through Welland, lined with industry (above) and next to the downtown core(below), has been retained as a recreational waterway.

ridges, shaped and moulded in order to provide a variety of landscapes. The ultimate hope (not yet fulfilled) is for extensive landscaping including 2 million trees and the creation of a major Federal or Provincial Park with recreation and camping facilities. A dock (Wharf 10) provided

Fred A. Addis

George Bayley, STELCO

Loading activity at the new Welland dock.

on the west bank to serve the City of Welland, provides the occasional venue for moored ships. It replaced industrial docks on the abandoned channel.

The By-Pass is almost straight and without overhead obstructions. Its width, 107 m (350 feet) at the bottom and 152 m (500 feet) at the surface with 3½:1 side slopes required a substantial cut in the landscape. Its construction across the eastern flank of Welland permitted the two way passage of ships by day or night along its 13.35 km (8.3 mile) length. Unlike the rest of the Canal, where generally only the west bank and certain sections of the east bank are illuminated, both banks are illuminated.

Two tunnels, one on Main Street for highway traffic and a combined highway/railway tunnel further south, take traffic under the new channel. Local roads that formerly crossed the Canal are closed, and rail tracks that crossed the previous channel were re-routed to the tunnel approaches by building about 160 km (100 miles) of new trackage. New stations, freight depots and marshalling yards were also constructed. As the grade adopted for the rail tracks was a slender .75 percent, a fall of only 22.86 cm (9 inches) for each 30.48 m (100 feet), the tracks occupy a cut which is about 4 km (2.5 miles) long on both sides of the By-Pass Channel.

The By-Pass has reduced the length of the Canal by about 1.29 km (.8 miles), almost doubled its width, and speeded the passage of ships. It also has important urban repercussions in that it placed the central part of the city and its eastern residential areas on a large man-made island, approached by two tunnels from the west and by fixed bridges in the east. Welland is accustomed to many such pertinent changes for its

John N. Jackson

The By-Pass Channel, a major engineering feat, was constructed between 1967 and 1973. The views are at Port Robinson looking north (above) and south (below).

St. Lawrence Seaway Authority

National Map Collection A24317-1200, 1976,
from University Map Library,
Department of Geography, Brock University

Welland sits on a man-made island between the winding channel of the Fourth Canal (left) and its new, straighter By-Pass Channel (right).

evolution, though the By-Pass and its implications are the largest in scale throughout its urban history. The Welland Public Library at 140 King Street, in downtown Welland next to the abandoned channel, might be visited for details of these changing circumstances.

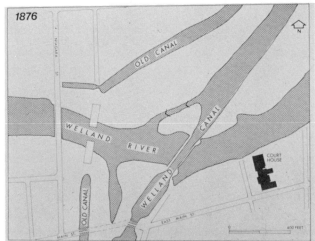

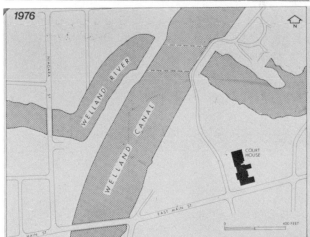

Department of Georgraphy, Brock University

The changing scene in downtown Welland. The water system at 1876 (above) and 1976 (below).

79

John N. Jackson
The Second Canal aqueduct preserved as a swimming
pool

2.9 Port Colborne and the Southern Length

A triple sequence of channels can be viewed and compared at Ramey's Bend. The By-Pass Channel meets the Fourth Canal, which here cuts across the Third Canal. The abandoned length of the Third Canal to the south contains a dry dock. The area is leased by a ship breaking firm for scrapping old vessels and by the Canadian Coast Guard for its Marine Emergency Duties Training Centre to train shipboard personnel in marine firefighting, rescue and survival techniques. The arm also provides a favoured spot for winter ice fishing.

Interestingly enough, on the west bank, the continuation of the abandoned Third Canal now serves as a raceway which supplies the modern Canal with water; the regulating weir is located under the bridge where Highway 3 crosses the Canal and changes from Main Street East to Main Street West. The northern entrance to this channel serves as a turning basin, where ships up to 168 m (550 feet) long may enter and leave the wharfage area of Robin Hood Mills from Lake Erie without passing through the Canal. The elevator and mills together provide a commanding vertical presence in the landscape of north Port Colborne. Usually with moored ships nearby, there is the perpetual reminder about the importance of the grain trade for Canada and the Welland Canal. The mill complex is served by rail and truck transport in addition to its shipping facilities.

John N. Jackson

The abandoned Third Canal at Ramey's Bend, Port Colborne, is used for the break-up of ships and as a winter recreational resource for ice fishing.

Fred A. Addis

The Robin Hood Mills, a remarkable industrial landscape, at Port Colborne.

An area on the west bank north of Robin Hood Mills was purchased in 1921 for the deposition of spoil excavated from the line of the Fourth Canal. It collected surface run-off and became known, ignominiously, as Mud Lake. However, after the gradual return and planting of vegetation, the 165-acre site is now managed for wildlife and public recreation by the Ontario Ministry of Natural Resources. A trail and board-walk provide access. Controlled waterfowl hunting is allowed each fall, and song birds, wading birds and waterfowl may each be observed throughout the year. 168 species have been recorded. Take Elm Street north from Highway 3 at Port Colborne or south from Forkes Road in Welland for access to this rather distinctive nature reserve.

As the water level of Lake Erie fluctuates with changes in wind direction, a guard lock is necessary to secure a steady working level of water for the Canal. It provides a shallow though variable lift and can, as it is located east of the Canal line rather than centrally, be duplicated if necessary. With a length of 420.6 m (1,380 feet) between the gates, Lock 8 is one of the largest in the world. Highway access to this facility is on the west bank south of Highway 3. A raised spectator viewing area, gardens and parking facilities are located immediately west of the lock. When water conditions permit, a *"walk-through"* procedure exists for ships; i.e. the vessel does not secure in the lock but proceeds through under its own power, with mooring lines being carried by lock personnel should mooring become necessary.

Downtown Port Colborne features moored vessels at all times of the year, because vessels berth at Port Colborne for off-season repairs and

St. Lawrence Seaway Authority

The southern lengths of the Canal system at Port Colborne. The former Third Canal (right) now serves as the hydraulic raceway for the present Canal.

there is the constant passage of ships during the navigation season. Extensive wharves line both banks up to the Clarence Street Bridge and beyond, and industrial activities on both banks are supplied with raw materials from the Canal.

West Street parallel to the Canal on its west bank contains many mid-nineteenth century buildings, and provides an active service venue for Canal and Lake activities that include oil bunkering, pilot services, Lake fishing vessels, ship suppliers and support industries. (East Street was removed to achieve the Third Canal.) Parts of the Second, Third and Fourth (or modern) Canal systems exist next to each other near the Clarence Street bridge. This bridge, No. 21, sits on lock walls of the Second and Third Canals. Urban renewal on West Street provides the pertinent reminder that urban character and the Canal are closely intertwined, one with the other. The Port Colborne Historical and Marine Museum, with Canal and city memorabilia, is nearby at 280 King Street. The Library, on the same street, might also be visited.

The Harbour has been extended gradually but sequentially over time into Gravelly Bay on Lake Erie. The location of former sand dunes can be recognized in the landscape by the slight rise of Sugarloaf Street. Here, a lock took the First Canal into Lake Erie. The west side now extends 1 km (.62 miles); the east side is longer at 1.52 km (.95 miles) and wider. The entrance has a controlling depth of 9.1 m (30 feet), which has been excavated into rock bottom. There are then the protective eastern and western breakwaters and their western extension, which enable ships to enter the Harbour and Canal even when a southwesterly gale is blowing. The

Fred A. Addis

Fred A. Addis

West Street, Port Colborne, a canal-oriented community since 1833.

breakwater foundations or cribbing were manufactured at Port Maitland on the Grand River about 50 km (30 miles) to the west, then towed and sunk in position on site. As these breakwaters enable the shallow western sections of Gravelly Bay to freeze over, the bay has become both a winter attraction for ice fishermen and a

The Port Colborne lighthouse, the southern point of entry to the Canal system.

protected area for summer marina facilities. Duck hunting is important in the Fall. The western breakwater also carries the Port Colborne lighthouse.

Both sides of the Harbour are lined extensively with industry, including such important companies as Marsh Engineering Limited, Bell Marine and Mill Supply Limited and Inco Metals.

Fred A. Addis

Port Colborne has more the appearance of a port than any other Canal community.

Upper Lakes Shipping has taken over the site owned by the Canadian Furnace Division of Algoma Steel. At the harbour entrance, are the Government Elevator operated by the National Harbours Board and the Maple Leaf Mills Elevator. The former, concerned with grain storage and transfer, used to be an important transfer point for Western grain before the Canal was enlarged and deepened; it now receives, handles and stores Ontario grain received by road. The Maple Leaf Mills, Robin Hood Multi Foods, and more recently Canada Starch to the north, combine grain storage with milling and processing. These mills serve as landmarks for mariners and within the urban environment. They provide a grand and pronounced entry to the Canal, the crowning features of the modern Harbour, and the reminder that the Welland Canal is a commercial waterway of considerable industrial importance.

Fred A. Addis

The impressive skyline of grain elevators and marina facilities at Gravelly Bay, Port Colborne.

2.10 Lest We Forget

Places other than along the route from Port Weller and Port Dalhousie to Port Colborne have associations with the Canal. A zone of historic interest along the Feeder Canal from the Grand River to Welland includes the villages of Wainfleet and Stromness that were created by the Canal, canal routes to Port Maitland where the Canal was locked down into the Grand River, and the Town of Dunnville where the Grand River was diverted towards the main line of the Canal by a dam. Power at the dam nurtured mill developments and provided the basis for a new industrial community that became the county town for the surrounding agricultural region. The system of navigation along the canalized Grand River, until the railway era, served into the Welland Canal via the Feeder Canal, and can be appreciated as part of the radiating system of canal waterways.

FEEDER BRIDGE, MARSHVILLE, ONT.

John Burtniak Collection

John N. Jackson

John Burtniak Collection

The Feeder Canal gave birth to, and shaped the character of, Wainfleet (above) and Dunnville (below).

Niagara-on-the-Lake (formerly Newark, then Niagara) lost its former status as the county seat to the upstart Canal towns of Welland and St. Catharines, and never recovered its former premier administrative and commercial role in the Peninsula. The Welland Canal communities were the new localities of expansion. The Canal introduced a new pattern of regional settlement into the Niagara Peninsula, replacing the former emphasis on the Niagara River and the portage communities.

Queenston and Chippawa, at the northern and southern ends of the portage around the Falls and at the head of navigation for their respective lengths of the Niagara River, survive as settlements that were important before the heyday of Canal supremacy. The overland portage that connected Queenston and Chippawa survives as Portage Road through Niagara Falls.

When the Welland Canal was constructed, Queenston was the first to suffer; Chippawa, at the mouth of the Welland River, was on the route of the original Welland Canal which, from 1829 to 1833, was routed along the Welland River and the Niagara River. When the Canal was extended to Port Colborne, the Welland River was made navigable for some 60 km (40 miles) upstream. The entrance to the Welland River at Chippawa was turned south for safety reasons; before this diversion, it used to flow into the Niagara River through the present site of King's Bridge Park.

Nor should the Short Hills, and villages like St. John's, be forgotten. Here wool, flour, timber and iron mills had created the major industrial centre of Upper Canada. As these mills could not compete with the regular flow of water that powered larger mills along the Canal, these communities slowly declined. The Canal, primarily an instrument of industrial progress, also displaced some former activities.

CANAL ENLARGEMENT!

At the request of the People a Public

MEETING

Has been called by the Mayor, and will be held at the

Town Hall, Clifton, Ont.,
FRIDAY, JANUARY 17, 1873.

To consider the subject of Canal enlargement, and to adopt measures to lay before the Government the advantages of the route from

CHIPPEWA TO QUEENSTON.

There can be no doubt this is the SHORTEST, CHEAPEST & BEST ROUTE for a Canal connecting the two Lakes Erie & Ontario. The present opportunity may never occur again, and therefore requires the

United, Earnest and Immediate Action
of the People of the Niagara Frontier.

The People of Niagara, Queenston, Clifton, Stamford, Chippewa, Willoughby, Bertie and Fort Erie, are especially Invited to Attend the Meeting, and the public generally are invited.

Turn Out En-Masse!

And let the Government and Country see that you are in earnest in this great and important matter.

CHAIR TO BE TAKEN AT 7·30 P. M.

St. Catharines Historical Museum

Despite attempts to the contrary, canals were not constructed between the Upper and Lower Niagara Rivers, or from Thorold to either Queenston or Niagara-on-the-Lake.

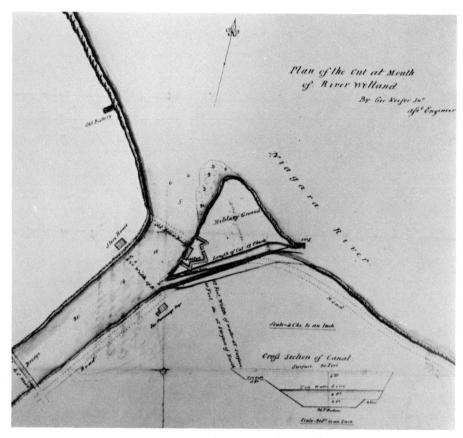

George Keefer, 1829, Ontario Archives,
from University Map Library,
Department of Geography, Brock University

The canal cut at Chippawa at the mouth of the Welland River.

III
Ships and Trade on the Canal

3.1 Ship Types

Many ships sail through the Canal, including the occasional highlight of a passenger vessel or warship. Specialized vessels include grey-hulled cement carriers, crane ships, tugs and barges. Sometimes a flotilla of small boats passes through the system, and there is the occasional

elegant yacht. Those with an everyday presence in the Canal include ships of the Great Lakes fleet, which are of three distinct types: those which carry dry bulk cargoes; those which carry liquid cargoes; and those carrying general cargo.

Historically the development of these lake

John N. Jackson

St. Lawrence Seaway Authority

The occasional passenger liner or naval vessel may be seen in the Canal.

ships or **"lakers"** has been closely linked and to a large extent governed by the parallel development of the Welland Canal. The limitations of size imposed by the dimensions of the locks on the Welland Canal are responsible for the maximum Seaway size bulk carrier as we know it today. Lake shippers, seeking to maximize the cubic cargo carrying capacity of their ships, have designed ships which conform to the Canal and lock limitations. These have produced ships which appear as virtual floating boxes, sharp cornered and perpendicular as the locks themselves.

The dry bulk cargo vessels are mainly of two types: the self-unloading bulk carrier or **"self-unloader"**, and the conventional bulk carrier sometimes called a **"flat-top"** or **"straight-decker"**. The self-unloader, through a series of cargo handling belts or bucket elevators, lifts the cargo from the ship's hold to a point above the

E.B. (Skip) Gillham

The Self-loading Bulk Carrier. How it works (below) and the Canadian Progress, launched in 1968 from Port Weller Dry Docks (above).

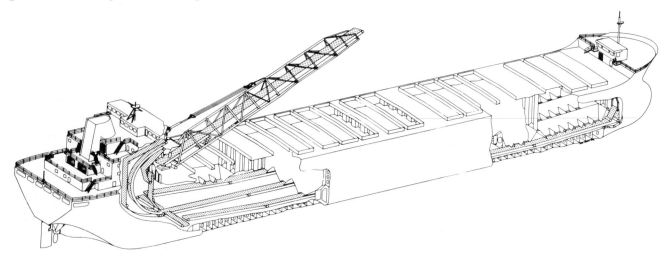

Self-Unloading Bulk Carrier

Port Weller Dry Docks

The Bulk Carrier, Carol Lake, at Port Colborne heading for Lake Erie.

deck level. It then deposits it on an unloading cargo boom which swings out when the ship is docked, and deposits the cargo on shore without shore-based assistance from either equipment or personnel. The newest ships of this type are capable of carrying 30,000 tonnes of cargo. They can unload at a rate of 6,000 tonnes of iron ore or 4,800 tonnes of coal per hour. Stone, salt and gypsum are other cargoes commonly carried by self-unloaders.

The conventional bulk carrier is the workhorse of the Canadian fleet using the Welland Canal. Their typical duties involve the transportation of grain to massive storage facilities on the St. Lawrence. It is then loaded onto deep sea vessels for overseas delivery. Returning upbound,

bulk carriers bring ore from Labrador and Quebec to Canadian and American steel mills on the lakes.

Both conventional bulk carriers and self-unloaders are limited in size to the dimensions of the Seaway locks. The largest ships on these routes are 222.50 m (730 feet) in length and handle about 25,000 tonnes of cargo. This is enough grain to make three loaves of bread for every man, woman and child in Canada. If this volume was carried by rail, it would require a train about 8 km (5 miles) long.

The Tanker carries bulk liquid petroleum and chemical cargoes. Imperial St. Clair was built at Port Weller Dry Docks.

Liquid cargoes on the lakes are carried by tankers. Small, efficient tankers make up the bulk of the Great Lakes fleet handling liquid cargo. Because of the availability of petroleum pipelines for most industrial needs, the small tankers service specialized industrial demands such as caustic soda for the Ontario Paper Company in Thorold and heating oil for Niagara's homes. Other tankers are in transit to and from refinery centres at Montreal, Toronto, Clarkson, Oakville or Sarnia. Grades of gasoline, diesel, kerosene, stove oil, and aviation fuel may be the cargo in the tanks of these vessels. U.S. tankers or tank barges also frequent the canal en route to U.S. ports, some trading to New York City via the New York State Barge Canal at Oswego.

John N. Jackson

A Tank Barge being pushed into Lock 7. Note the elevated wheelhouse on the tug for visibility reasons.

The package freight fleet is declining, yet still provides a valuable service through Canada Steamship Lines. Their "Fort Class" ships provide a regular link between terminal facilities at Valleyfield, Hamilton, Windsor, Sarnia, Sault Ste. Marie and Thunder Bay. Most package freighters feature a *"tween decks"* or intermediate deck between the main deck and bottom of the cargo hold. Through *"ports"* (doors) in the ship's side, palletized, mixed cargo is handled by forklift trucks.

E.B. (Skip) Gillham

The Package Freighter, Fort Chambly, was built at Collingwood, Ontario, in 1961.

The opening of the Seaway in 1959 allowed much of the world's ocean fleet to reach inland ports on the Great Lakes. These *"salties"* provide a regular link with European, African and Asian centres, and carry a variety of raw materials and manufactured goods. In recent years containerized cargoes have been gaining an increasingly important share of the market. Many deep sea callers are in search of grain cargoes. They load to the maximum Seaway depth and then *"top off"* at St. Lawrence ports. Some salties return year after year to become *"regulars"* on the Canal scene. Others may make but one trip.

E.B. (Skip) Gillham

Typical Salties, with cabins aft. The Orion (above), built in
1963, has sailed under Greek and Liberian flags. The
Biban (below), with cargo-handling cranes, in ballast.

Fred A. Addis

Hugh J Gayler

The end of an era: an old lake steamboat heads towards
Lake Ontario. Regulations now prohibit this type of smoke
emission from vessels on the Canal.

Before entering the Seaway, salties must meet
equipment requirements unique to the system.
These include proper markings for draught and
bulbous bow; fenders to protect Seaway installa-
tions from any protruding part of a vessel's
structure; landing booms and mooring lines;
radio telephones with proper Seaway frequen-
cies; and an on-board sewage disposal system.

3.2 Ship Terminology

The *"landlubber"* (a person unfamiliar with either the sea or shipping) must know certain words and phrases to understand a ship, because every profession uses technical terms to describe its specialized work. Those used by the seaman have sometimes become part of the English language, and often terms and phrases in marine usage have enjoyed hundreds of years of tradition in their usage. They are complicated on the Welland Canal, as both lake vessels (lakers) and sea-going vessels (salties) are involved.

The words *"ship"*, *"boat"* and *"vessel"* tend to be used interchangeably. A *"ship"* is the generic name for sea-going vessels, as opposed to *"boats"* which are generally small open craft without any decks; exceptions include a tug boat and a fishing boat. A *"vessel"* is the term used officially, for example in the Tariff and Tolls by the Seaway Authority where it means *"every type of craft used as a means of transportation on water."*

The essential elements of a ship include a *"stem"* to form the *"bow"* or front end, and a *"stern"* or after end, attached to a *"keel"*. The keel is the lowest continuous line of a ship extending the whole length of a vessel; it is the spine or backbone of a ship, and is the strongest single unit because it must support the weight of the ship irrespective of wave length and height. The *"ribs"* or frame of a ship are attached to the keel and thereby shape the *"hull"*, which is the main surface body of a ship but excluding its masts, sails, yards and rigging.

The hull is divided into *"fore"* (front), *"midship"* (middle), and *"aft"* (rear) parts. A line running lengthways along the ship runs from fore to aft, stem to stern, with the right side facing the *"bow"* (stem) being *"starboard"* and the left side facing the bow being *"port"*. The starboard side carries a green light and the port side a red light. The rule of the *"road"* (right-of-way) is that, when two vessels approach end-on, each gives way to the other by turning to starboard (right), so that they pass on their port (left-hand) sides. This explains why, at the Flight Locks, vessels pass down on the right (eastern) side, and rise on the left (western) side.

When the ship is *"afloat"* (waterborne) there is a division between the *"ship's side"* above the waterline and the *"bottom"* below water level. This introduces the concept of a *"plimsoll"* mark or load line, and the weird hieroglyphics that appear on the hull of every ship that

Fred A. Addis

A Lake Erie fish tug (right) and pilot boat (left) in harbour ice at Port Colborne.

sails through the Welland Canal. It is seen *"amidship"* (centrally) at or near the water line of a ship. The notation indicates the depth to which the ship may legally be loaded. It is higher for fresh water than for sea water, because of

their differences in *"displacement"* (the weight of a ship indicated by the tonnes of water she displaces when loaded and afloat).

Various terms are applied to the hull of a ship. *"Freeboard"* is the distance between the

The hull of a ship under construction at Port Weller Dry Docks reveals its structure.   Port Weller Dry Docks

waterline and the uppermost deck that is water-tight. **"Beam"** is the greatest width of the hull, and **"camber"** is the actual surface or slope of the deck so that water will drain into the **"scuppers"** or openings on the side of the ship to allow the run-off of surplus water. **"Keel"** is the central part, underwater, of the ship, the **"bilge"** the flat bottom of the hull centred on the keel, and the **"draught"** of a ship is the depth of the keel below the waterline.

Port Weller Dry Docks

Port Weller Dry Docks
Ship names and markings at the bow.

Draught marks can be seen at the bow, stern and amidship of a ship, indicating the depth of water which a ship is **"drawing"** at any particular time. Many lake ships bear both feet and metric draught marks, the depth being indicated by the lower end of the painted roman or arabic numerals.

Some ships are marked with the **"bowthruster"** symbol, usually at the bow of the ship. It indicates that the ship is equipped with a bowthruster and serves as a warning to small craft moving about the ship. The bowthruster is an independent propeller installed **"athwartship"** (across the ship) to assist a large ship in moving laterally in confined waters such as the Canal. This assembly virtually eliminates the need for tugs to assist in docking the largest of lake ships.

Another marking at the bow of the ship indicates a projection, usually in the shape of a bulb that projects below the waterline at the bow. The marking serves as a warning to other vessels so as not to foul the ships bow, the bulbous portion being below the waterline when the ship is loaded.

The ship itself contains **"decks"**, a series of horizontal platforms that extend in tiers from one side of the ship to the other. The **"forecastle"** traditionally for the crew is in front of the main mast, and the **"poop"** or **"quarter deck"** is the after part of the upper deck usually reserved for officers. The **"hold"** is the interior of the ship below decks where the cargo is stored. This area is divided into separate compartments for safety reasons by upright, vertical partitions known as **"bulkheads"**. Access to these holds is by **"hatches"** through which the cargo is hoisted or lowered. This may be by **"derricks"** or cranes on the ship, or from cranes on land.

The seaman lives **"in"** not on a ship. He arrives **"aboard"** or **"on board"**, and the ship **"ties up"** and then **"lays alongside"** a wharf or dock wall. He goes to his **"mess"** (living quarters) on the **"messdeck"** through a **"hatch"** (door), and ascends or descends a **"ladder"** (stairway) to other spaces on the ship. Walls are **"bulkheads"**, the floor is the **"deck"**, and the ceiling is the **"deckhead"**. A ship is **"under way"** when it is neither anchored, nor secured to a buoy or quay. She has **"way"** on her when moving through water. When moving forward she is **"making headway"** or **"going ahead"**, moving backwards she is **"going astern"**, or **"making sternway"**, and moving sideways is to move **"broadside"** to port or starboard.

The tonnage of a ship is expressed in various ways. The **"avoirdupois ton"** is equal to 2,240 pounds (the **"long ton"**), in contrast with the U.S. avoirdupois ton, equal to 2,000 pounds (the **"short ton"**). The **"tonne"**, now used by the St. Lawrence Seaway Authority for the assessment of tolls and in their statistical presentations, is the metric ton equivalent of 1,000 kilograms (2,204.62 pounds). Measurements of a ship's tonnage include **"gross tonnage"**, the total weight of the vessel, and **"net registered tonnage"**, its cubic capacity for carrying cargo.

The St. Lawrence Seaway Authority uses certain definitions for their Tariff of Tolls for a vessel to **"transit"** (pass through) the canals and locks of the system. **"Bulk cargo"** means goods that are loose or in mass and which must generally be shovelled, pumped, blown, scooped or forked in handling; they include cement, coke, liquids, ores and minerals, pig iron and scrap metal, raw sugar, and woodpulp. **"Containerized cargo"** means any general cargo shipped in enclosed, permanent, reusable, nondisposable, weather-tight shipping conveyances with a cubic capacity of 209.97 m (640 feet) or more, and fitted with a minimum of one hinged door. **"Feed grains"** means barley, corn, oats, flaxseed, rapeseed, soybeans and other oilseeds. **"Food grains"** means buckwheat, dried beans, dried peas, rye and wheat.

A ship sails **"in ballast"** when it carries no cargo, but some heavy material may be placed in the hold to secure stability. With cargo volumes not being uniform in both directions, this feature has flavoured local townscape features because, when early ships brought in stone or brick as ballast, this material could be used in building construction. For example, the larger and older section of the Niagara Apothecary on Queen Street in Niagara-on-the-Lake is faced with limestone from the Kingston area.

Finally, why is ship feminine and referred to as **"she"** or **"her"** even if it is named after a man? This tradition dates back to the sixteenth century, but the precise reasons are unknown. According to E.C. Russell, ***Customs and Traditions in the Canadian Armed Forces: "The most likely explanation ... is the traditional belief of sailors that a Ship is very close to being a living entity, endowed with spirit and a distinct personality, demanding respect and, given proper consideration, most dependable. And, somehow, through some curious alchemy in the mind of the seaman in the days of sail, often away from the land for months on end, this near-human being took on the beauty and mystique of a woman."***

3.3 Canadian Shipping

More than 175 vessels are operated by the 20 member companies of the Dominion Marine Association (Suite 703, 350 Sparks Street, Ottawa). This fleet has an overall carrying capacity of more than 3.2 million tonnes, represents over $1 billion in investment, and carries annually cargo on the lakes worth $7 billion. The Dominion Marine Association employs more than 6,000 crew and on-shore staff, with a payroll exceeding $100 million a year. While entirely a Canadian industry, it is, nevertheless, largely dependent on world markets and has to compete with heavily subsidized industries in other nations, notably Japan which can undercut world prices by up to 50 per cent.

In terms of exports, Canada ranks seventh in the world's use of ocean transport. In recent years exports and imports by water, excluding those to the U.S., have totalled more than $30 billion. In spite of this, Canada has only a small foreign-going fleet and Association members are anxious to see it increase. As a result, its member companies are becoming increasingly involved in overseas shipping, largely in an attempt to offset the winter freezeup on the Lakes which leaves expensive ships idle. However, this requires special modifications so that ships can sail the Lakes and the high seas.

Fred A. Addis

Ship markings denote the ownership of vessels. This one belongs to Halco Inc., Westmount, Quebec.

3.4 Flags

A ship *"wears"* the ensign of her nationality, either on the *"Ensign Staff"* on the *"taffrail"* or rail around the stern (i.e. the aftermost part of the ship), or on the peak of the *"main gaff"* or *"steaming gaff"*. This ensign should either be *"close up"* (i.e. fully hoisted) or at *"half mast"* (i.e. about one-third of the distance down from the uppermost point). A flag worn at half mast is a signal of mourning, usually for a crew member, or a dignitary of the ship's own nationality or that of the country which she is visiting.

A ship will often *"fly"* a *"house flag"* at the main mast or highest point on board. This flag is the one adopted by the owners to signify vessels of the same fleet. It is sometimes very similar in colours and pattern to the colours and pattern on the *"funnel"* (smoke stack). Apart from the company flag, a ship may fly *"courtesy flags"*; the provincial, municipal and the St. Lawrence Seaway flags can frequently be seen.

Other flags that are flown are from an international code of signal flags. They inform other ships and shore stations about the nature of the ship, its intentions, or her cargo.

Some of the more commonly used flags are:

A) A burgee (swallow-tailed flag) divided vertically, white at the hoist (mast) and blue at the fly, means *"I am undergoing speed trials"*. This could be used by a ship leaving the Port Weller Dry Docks for speed trials on Lake Ontario.

B) An all red burgee known as the danger flag means *"I am taking in, or discharging, or carrying explosives, oil or fuels"*. Loaded tankers will often fly this flag.

G) A flag with yellow and blue vertical bars denotes that the ship requires a Pilot.

H) A vertically divided flag, white at the hoist and red at the fly, signifies *"I have a Pilot aboard"*.

O) A red and yellow diagonally divided flag means *"Man overboard"*.

P) A blue flag with a white square in the centre, the *"Blue Peter"*, means (when flown in harbour) that *"the vessel is about to proceed to Sea"*.

Q) An all yellow flag known as the quarantine flag means *"My vessel is healthy and I request free pratique (entry to port)"*.

The position of these flags shows their importance, the most important place being the main mast, then from the starboard (right) yard arm inwards, followed by the port (left) yard arm inwards. By combining two or more of the signal flags whole messages can be transmitted, but today the *"very high frequency"* radio telephone has virtually taken over the exchange of information between ships, or between ships and shore stations.

3.5 Ship Names and Registration

Ship names are as many and various as the individual ships which bear them. The age old tradition of naming ships after members of the female gender is not generally applied in these modern times. A ship is usually named at a launching or christening ceremony, with the actual name reflecting some aspect of the operation of the ship owners.

Some companies have theme names which run through their fleet such as *Canadian Transport, Canadian Enterprise* and *Canadian Pioneer.* Other fleets will use a particular suffix or prefix in their ship names such as *Algosoo, Algoport* and *Algowood* which are ships of the Algoma Central Marine fleet, honouring Sault Ste. Marie, Port Colborne and Collingwood respectively, as cities having particular interest in the company's operations.

Ships can be named for the cargoes they carry such as *Chemical Transport;* for the rivers they ply such as *Saguenay, St. Lawrence, Richelieu;* for company executives such as *E. B. Barber, Robert S. Pierson, Louis R. Desmarais;* and by virtually any other criteria.

A ship's name is by law displayed at the bow and stern of the ship, but most ships also carry nameboards at either side of the wheelhouse. On many ocean vessels the names at the bow and wheelhouse will be in English characters, while those at the stern are often in the language of the vessel's home port of registry.

A ship's port of registry is displayed beneath the name at the stern. Each ship by law must have a home port and subscribe to the particular maritime laws for operation and safety which are adhered to in the country of that port. The port of registry does not always indicate the nationality or ownership of a ship. Some shipowners prefer to register their ships in countries where maritime laws are less strict than perhaps their own. *"Flags of convenience"* is the term used to describe this registration policy.

John N. Jackson

The ships of many nations traverse the Canal. Where is this one from?

100

Goods produced next to the Canal may be transported to their destination in vessels that are named and registered abroad.

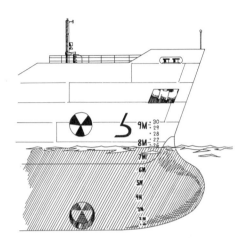

Markings at the bow of a typical ship indicate (from left to right) a bowthruster, used to propel the ship sideways in confined waters; a bulbous bow below the waterline to warn small craft such as tugs moving close to the ship's bow; and draught marks showing the vessel's depth in the water, first measured in meters and then feet.

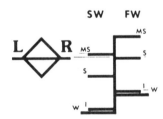

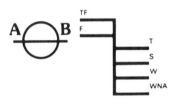

KEY

LR Lloyd's Registry (authorized licensing body)
SW Salt Water
FW Fresh Water
MS Mid-summer Load Line
S Summer Load Line
I Intermediate Load Line
W Winter Load Line

KEY

AB American Bureau of Shipping (authorized licensing body)
TF Tropical Fresh Water Allowance
F Fresh Water Allowance
T Load Line in Tropical Zones
S Summer Load Line
W Winter Load Line
WNA Winter North Atlantic Load Line

Plimsoll or Load Line markings for ocean going vessels (right) and a typical laker (left) are displayed at mid-length of a ship at or near the waterline. These marks indicate the depth to which a vessel may be loaded during certain seasons and in different waters.

3.6 The Pilot and His Duties

Not all ships that pass through the Canal have to carry a Pilot. The Captain of the domestic ships or *"laker"* is usually well-acquainted with the Canal and other waters of the Great Lakes, and is not obliged to take on a Pilot. He is his own Pilot. However, the Captain of the ocean freighter or *"saltie"*, whilst being able to navigate in *"great waters"* does not visit the Great Lakes frequently enough to become familiar with the peculiarities of the Canal and river passages, and thus by regulation **must** take a Pilot. Generally speaking, the *"saltie"* will wear a foreign flag, whilst the *"laker"* wears the Canadian or United States flag.

The cost of Pilot services is paid by the owners or operators of a ship according to a published scale of fees or tariff. The fees vary with the size of the ship, the distance that a ship is under the advice of a Pilot, and certain other services that a Pilot may peform such as docking or undocking a vessel. Because a Pilot is a skilled professional, these fees are quite high. For example an average size ship would be charged approximately $1,500.00 in 1980 for a full transit of the Welland Canal, but the loss in time and cost of possible repairs could far exceed this fee if the conduct of the ship was left in the hands of a less skilled Mariner without experience of the Canal.

Pilots in the Canal are under the direction and regulations of the Great Lakes Pilotage Authority, Ltd., a Crown Company, and form part of Great Lakes District Number 2. The Pilots group themselves into a body, known since earliest times as a Corporation. Usually a Mariner who enters the Pilot Service has spent all his sea-going career in and around the Great Lakes. But even if he started his working life many miles away from the Great Lakes, he is only accepted because of a wide experience within the waters in which he is to be a Pilot.

A Pilot receives his Licence only after examination and a period of practical on-the-job training since, although he is fully conversant with the Canal, he has to learn the differences in the handling characteristics of salties from the lakers he has been used to. This demanding requirement results in a proud profession exemplified by the statement: *"Your true Pilot cares nothing about anything on Earth but the Canal, and his pride in his occupation surpasses the pride of Kings"* (after the style of Mark Twain, referring originally to the Mississippi River).

Because a Pilot is highly experienced in the waters for which he is licensed, he is engaged as an adviser by the Captain of a vessel whose knowledge of the Canal is limited. As in practice it would be very cumbersome for a Pilot to tell the Captain of the ship what he is best advised to do and then for the Captain to instruct his crew, the Pilot takes charge of the ship and crew as far as the navigation through the Canal is concerned and thus assumes the same authority as the Captain. It is the Pilot's job to make all the orders of engine speed and steering, and also to order the crew in the procedures of docking and undocking. Again, because of his familiarity with the area, the Pilot maintains the necessary radio communications with the Canal Control Centre, the Marine Traffic Stations and other ships in the vicinity.

The Pilot comes Aboard.

Drawn for this book by Captain Leroy Pero, Canal Pilot, District No. 2

Conning a ship is not an exact science. It calls for a fine sense of judgement, based on many years of practical experience. Ships cannot be braked to a standstill like an automobile. They are at the vagaries of the wind and at the mercy of the water currents. In order to steer, a ship must be moving forward—the expression is *"to have steerage way on her"*. In order to stop a ship, the engine has to be reversed but this poses problems. Ships do not steer when going astern but rather develop a turning motion, normally to starboard (right) or clockwise.

Also, when a ship gets close to the bank of the Canal, she reacts in different ways than if she were in the middle of the channel. A Pilot is aware of all these factors and uses them to his advantage. To the casual onlooker on the bank, a ship may appear to be heading in a strange direction or executing an odd manoeuvre. In fact, everything is very much under the control of the professional *"man at the helm"*, the Pilot.

3.7 The Movement and Control of Vessels

With ever increasing traffic generated by the completion of the Seaway along the St. Lawrence, the Welland Canal experienced a serious problem in 1964. Demand on the system (vessel arrival rate) came dangerously close to capacity service rate, and delays resulting from large queues of vessels at each end of the Welland Canal became chronic. A co-ordinated modernization program introduced improvements in operating methods, that included a sophisticated Traffic Control Centre at the Seaway administrative headquarters in St. Catharines. Equipment installed in a large control console comprised:

- closed circuit T.V. monitors with remote camera controls which could survey all major sections and structures along the

St. Lawrence Seaway Authority

Inside the St. Lawrence Seaway Authority's Traffic Control Centre on Glendale Avenue, St. Catharines.

Canal.
- mimic lock display units which indicated water/hardware/navigation/light activity via direct instant telemetry.
- lockage timers to measure the performance of vessel's entry, locking and exit times.
- an animated display board reflecting pertinent information and locations of vessel traffic within the Canal system.
- improved V.H.F. marine radio telephone system.
- continuous read-out instruments showing wind velocity 'and direction from various locations along the Canal.
- an automatic radio log for the retention of all communications pertinent to navigation as required by law.
- *"hard copy"* communication machines and direct line telephones.

The system has later been expanded to include:

- additional remotely operated radio stations.
- traffic control extended into the eastern portion of Lake Erie and the western half of Lake Ontario, later modified in these areas and along the Canal to a *"computer assisted"* system.
- microwave detection units to track vessels along the Welland By-Pass.
- remotely controlled variable intensity

lighting along the summit level to assist vessels during periods of reduced visibility.

- silicon and silicon intensified target C.C.T.V. cameras to improve night viewing capabilities.
- visibility and weather monitoring instrumentation at Port Robinson.

The St. Lawrence Seaway Authority estimates that Traffic Control has increased Canal capacity somewhere in the order of 20 percent. Regretfully, because of limited viewing space, the Control Centre can be viewed only by making special advance arrangements with the Authority. Perhaps one day the details can be relayed to some external viewing point, and thereby become a featured attraction.

Along the Canal, signs with the letters L/A (limit of approach) are located at the approaches to locks and movable bridges to assist the vessel master in his approach. The system consists of a navigation signal light panel with three warning L/A signs along the approach wall of each end of

John N. Jackson

The approach to a lock.

the lock. The lights are operated from the control room of the lock.

Light panels are displayed at the end of each lock (except between the flight locks). Their purpose is to indicate to an approaching vessel the state of readiness of the lock. The mode of operation of the lights indicates the dumping or filling of the lock, whether one or more vessels are in the lock, and whether the approaching vessel will be handled next or held at the wall.

A fixed red light means that the lock is occupied; do not pass the illuminated L/A. Red flashing lights mean that the lock is occupied, but stand by to move into the lock when the outbound vessel(s) has passed you; red flashing together means one vessel, and red flashing alternately means more than one vessel.

Each fixed amber light means two minutes of time, and each flashing amber light means one minute of time. The lights go out in sequence starting from the top of the panel, with the last being extinguished when the end of the lock becomes fully open. By counting the amber lights, it is therefore possible to determine the period until the lock is fully open, e.g. two fixed amber and one flashing amber mean five minutes until the upper end is fully open.

Green lights mean that the lock is ready to receive a ship; enter as promptly as possible. Reduction of *"dead time"*, the period between the exit of one vessel and the entry of the other, is imperative to increase the traffic capacity of the Canal as its volume of flow increases.

Movement through the Canal is for 24 hours a day through the navigation season. Navigation is closed or reduced to one way operations when visibility is unsafe for navigation, or high winds prevail.

Mile Posts indicating nautical miles are located at one mile intervals along the entire length of the Canal commencing at Port Weller. They are located on the west bank. Ships will often refer to the mile posts when reporting their position while proceeding through the Canal.

The sign for submerged cable indicates those points at which electrical transmission cables and sundry gas, water and sewer lines pass under the Canal. The sign serves as a warning to mariners that they must not drop anchor in such positions, as this could foul the cables.

Whistle signals may also be heard and, as in ports the world over, become sound effects in the urban environment. Even in this day of electronics and radio, a ship is required to give certain audible signals on her whistle to indicate both her presence and actions in times of fog, snow and other limitations of visibility. Since a ship could not transit the Canal in bad visibility, these signals are very rarely heard within the Canal but are used on the open lakes; however, over the years, Captains and Pilots have come to use a single short blast on the whistle to tell the crew to *"cast off"* (let go) all the lines holding the ship to the shore or lock wall. Two short blasts indicate that the ship is *"in place"* along a lock approach wall or dock, and can now be securely moored by putting the lines on bollards. Listen for these signals next time you see a ship entering or leaving a dock.

Other ships sounds may be heard, including:

- An upbound and downbound vessel meeting in a channel: one blast from each vessel means that *"I am altering my course to starboard (right) and will pass on the port (left) side"*.
- Two blasts from each vessel mean *"I am altering my course to port (left) and will pass you on the starboard (right) side"*.
- A vessel proceeding in fog: three blasts every minute. Danger signal: five or more rapid blasts.

3.8 Vessel Operating Costs

Ships are expensive pieces of equipment, both to purchase and to operate.

Data supplied by a representative shipping company, in 1981, has indicated the daily operating cost for a large-sized laker approximates $11,000.00. These operating costs can be broken down into the categories of cargo expenses, salaries, wages and benefits, fuel costs, supplies, repairs and maintenance, and other operating costs.

Cargo expenses run from $1,600.00 to $1,700.00 per day depending on the type of cargo, the source and destination of the cargo, and the amount of overtime required to load and unload the vessel. Included in cargo expenses are Canal tolls which average out to about $250.00 per day.

Crew costs per ship depend upon the crew complement, which can range between 25 and 29. The average cost per man per day is approximately $125.00.

Fuel costs vary, depending mainly on whether the vessel is diesel or steam powered, but can run from $3,800.00 to $4,800.00 per day, with diesel engines being the more fuel efficient. Port days as well as navigating days are included in calculating the daily average.

Supplies, repairs and maintenance charges differ between diesel and steam plants, with diesel plants generally requiring more maintenance. The average supplies, repairs and maintenance charges can run from $1,000.00 to $1,400.00 per day.

Other operating costs include the cost of various vessel related insurance and a provision for the costs incurred to ensure the vessel passes its survey tests every five years. These costs average out to $700.00 per day. Vessel depreciation and on-shore administration and indirect costs are not included in the above operating costs.

3.9 Trade and Traffic

Traffic on the Welland Canal is classified to five major groups: grain; iron ore; coal; other bulk such as coke, petroleum, stone and salt; and general cargo, mostly iron and steel products. In 1980, about 60 million tonnes of cargo were carried on the Canal, with 47.6 million tonnes moving downbound and 12.0 million tonnes upbound. Vessel transits totalled 6,596; 4,968 lakers and 1,628 salties. 70.2 percent of vessels were Canadian by country of registry; the next highest percentages were Greece, the United States, Liberia and Yugoslavia, each with over 100 vessel transits.

Cargo movements in tonnes (1 tonne = 1,000 kilograms = 1.1023 short tons or .9482 long tons) during 1979 and 1980 were:

	UP 1980	DOWN 1980	TOTAL 1980	TOTAL 1979
Grain	–	28.1	28.1	26.2
Iron Ore	7.3	4.1	11.4	15.1
Coal	–	7.3	7.3	7.8
Other Bulk	3.5	7.7	11.2	13.9
General Cargo	1.2	0.4	1.6	3.3
	12.0	47.6	59.6	66.3

Grain is primarily a downbound movement of U.S. and Canadian exports from the Upper Great Lakes, destined as an export product for Europe and the U.S.S.R. Most is carried by bulk laker carriers to ports on the lower St. Lawrence River where it is trans-shipped mainly to foreign, ocean-going vessels, some is carried direct to foreign ports, and a smaller part is for domestic use at port centres such as Toronto and Montreal.

Iron ore movements reflect the major sources of supply, upstream near Lake Superior and downstream in Quebec and Labrador. There is an upbound traffic from Quebec and Labrador to Buffalo, Chicago, Nanticoke and U.S. ports south of Lake Erie, combined with a smaller downbound volume from ports on Lake Superior to steel works at Hamilton. This criss-crossing of the same product results from cost differences, variations in quality of the iron ore, and the varied needs of different steel producers.

Coal is primarily a downbound cargo. It includes metallurgical coal from U.S. ports south of Lake Erie to steel mills at Hamilton, and thermal coal destined for coal-fired generating stations operated by Ontario Hydro on the northern side of Lake Ontario.

Other bulk commodities might include coke upbound from foreign destinations to U.S. steel mills, the delivery of petroleum products from Canadian refineries at Sarnia or Toronto to the smaller markets and industrial consumers, sulphur from Alberta downbound to overseas destinations, and salt downbound from Goderich and Windsor for winter use on roads and in industrial processes. General cargoes of packaged items and containerized goods include scheduled services transporting packaged freight and containerized products between U.S. Great Lakes ports and abroad.

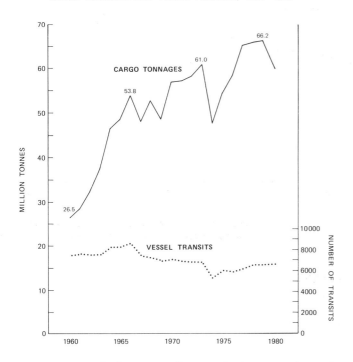

CARGO TONNAGES AND VESSEL TRANSITS, 1960 – 1980

St. Lawrence Seaway Authority, redrawn by Department of Geography, Brock University

Cargo tonnages and vessel transits on the Welland Canal, 1960-1980.

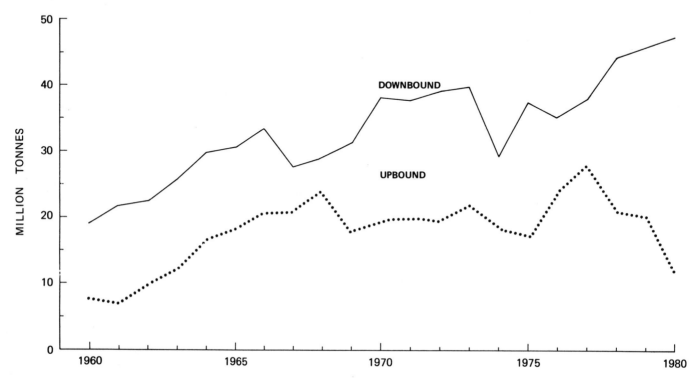

UPBOUND AND DOWNBOUND TRAFFIC, 1960 – 1980

MILLION TONNES

DOWNBOUND

UPBOUND

St. Lawrence Seaway Authority, redrawn by
Department of Geography, Brock University

Upbound and downbound cargo traffic on the Welland Canal, 1960-1980.

SELECTED COMMODITIES, 1960 – 1980

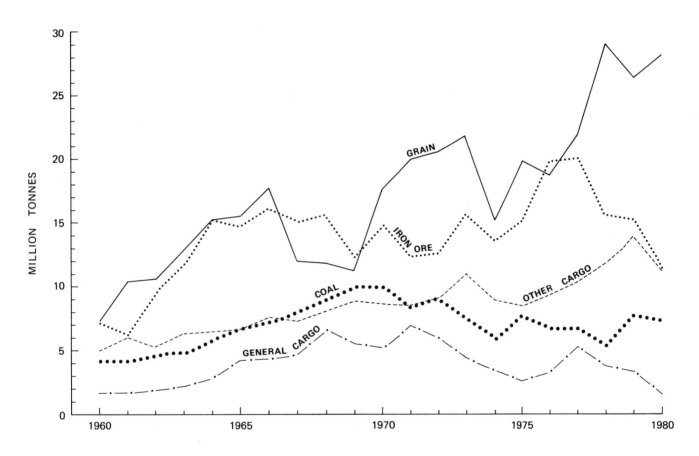

St. Lawrence Seaway Authority, redrawn by
Department of Geography, Brock University

Trends in the tonnes carried of the major bulk cargoes, 1960-1980.

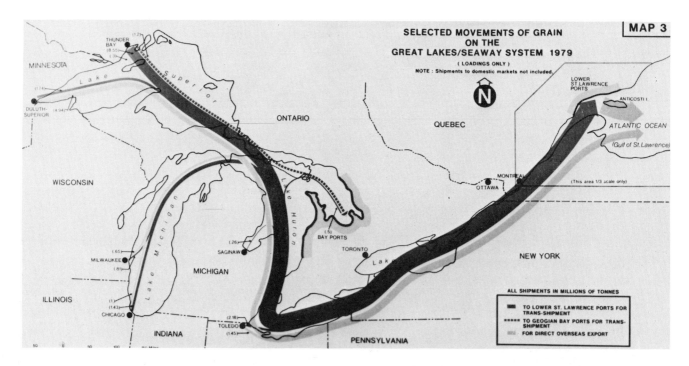

SELECTED MOVEMENTS OF GRAIN
ON THE
GREAT LAKES/SEAWAY SYSTEM 1979
(LOADINGS ONLY)
NOTE : Shipments to domestic markets not included.

MAP 3

ALL SHIPMENTS IN MILLIONS OF TONNES

TO LOWER ST. LAWRENCE PORTS FOR TRANS-SHIPMENT
TO GEORGIAN BAY PORTS FOR TRANS-SHIPMENT
FOR DIRECT OVERSEAS EXPORT

The pattern of cargo movement for grain, a major export product.

Ralph S. Misener, Provincial/Great Lakes
Seaway Task Force

John N. Jackson

Containerised cargo from Manchester, England, upbound
in the flight locks.

En route at Port Colborne from the Thorold dock to Port Stanley, and destined for Labatt's Brewery, London.

3.10 Tolls and Wharfage Charges

In order to meet daily operational costs and finance improvement projects, the St. Lawrence Seaway Authority levies tolls against a ship, its cargo and/or passengers. Two components are involved: a charge of $0.07 per gross registered tonne, applicable whether the vessel is wholly or partly laden, or in ballast; and a charge per metric ton of cargo, $0.50 for general cargo, and $0.31 for bulk and containerized cargoes, food and feed grains. A vessel making a partial transit of the Canal pays 13 percent of the applicable toll for each lock through which it passes. The charge per passenger is $6.00. Pleasure craft pay $4.00 per lock transited, with this rising to $8.00 for other vessels. The income yielded by tolls was $23.6 million in 1980, and other income was $2.2 million, against operating costs of $32.4 million for the Welland section of the Seaway, a net income loss of $6.6 million.

Users of the Seaway, represented by the Great Lakes Waterway Development Association (Suite 606, 116 Albert Street, Ottawa), have objected to tolls, lockage fees and their increasing impact, because *"they are discriminatory and inhibit transit of shipping and cargo vital to the economy"*. A 1978 statement has noted that other inland navigable waterways in North America are not currently subject to *"user-pay"* charges, that tolls directly affect competiveness, and that increasing the price of commodities passing through the Canal represents an invidious distinction against certain industries.

A differing viewpoint *(The St. Lawrence Sea-*

way and Its Regional Impact, Ministry of Supply and Services, Ottawa, 1979) is that the Seaway has considerably reduced shipping costs: *"The cost of shipping wheat from Thunder Bay to Quebec in 1975 was reduced by 15*

Fred Campbell Collection

Frank Allen, in Fred A. Addis Collection

Vessels in transit through the Canal pay tolls based on the registered tonnage of the vessel, the tonnes of cargo that are carried, and the number of locks through which they pass.

cents a bushel, or $5.00 per short ton. In 1976, the rate for shipping iron ore from Quebec-Labrador to Ontario and the U.S. was cut by $2.23 per long ton, and rates for coal, loaded in American ports on Lake Erie and shipped to Ontario ports on Lake Erie, fell by $2.70 per short ton.''

As shippers and the St. Lawrence Seaway Authority are both struggling to retain their viability, the issue of tolls will probably be subject to ongoing negotiation and revision for years to come. The Dominion Marine Association stress continually that the viability of shipping must be maintained as it is the most energy efficient mode of transport. They state that one gallon of fuel will take 1 ton of cargo 600 miles by ship, 200 miles by rail, 70 miles by truck, and 6 miles by air. Shipping a tonne of grain from Thunder Bay to Quebec City costs $22 by rail and $10 by ship. In recent years ships have carried more tonnes of freight per mile than either of the two major Canadian rail systems, despite the limitations of an eight- to nine-month navigation system as compared to year-round rail operations.

Apart from tolls, certain other charges are levied. *"Top Wharfage",* a charge on goods unloaded from or loaded onto vessels except for grain and grain products destined for export from Canada, is levied at $0.13 per tonne for bulk cargo and $0.30 per tonne for general cargo. Storage charges for goods on land owned by the Seaway Authority are $0.16 per square metre (m² or 1.1960 square yards) of area after the first 48 hours. *"Side Wharfage",* a charge based on the period of time a vessel is loading, unloading and lying in wait in the Canal, is

$0.0225 per gross registered tonne each day or part after the first 48 hours.

A vessel laying up in authorized areas of the Canal is charged $0.03 per gross registered tonne for every 30 days or part thereof. Based on the last figure, a maximum sized laker of 23,400 gross registered tonnes would be levied a charge of $2,106 for winter lay up along the Canal for a 90-day period, December 31st to March 31st.

Denis Cahill, St. Catharines Standard

In 1979, to celebrate 150 years of navigation on the Welland Canal, actor David MacKenzie (left), became a reincarnation of William Hamilton Merritt, founder of the Canal. He here exchanges top hat greetings with Captain George Potter (right) of the motor vessel H. M. Griffith.

IV
Canal Data and Information

4.1 The St. Lawrence Seaway Authority

Canals in Canada have a long history, culminating in 1951 when the Federal Government passed an Act to establish The St. Lawrence Seaway Authority for constructing, maintaining and operating, either wholly in Canada or in conjunction with the United States, a deep draft waterway between the Port of Montreal and Lake Erie. Then, in May 1954, the United States Congress authorized an American agency to build the navigation facilities required in United States territory in the international Rapids section of the St. Lawrence River. The project was completed five years later, and through transit of the Seaway began in April 1959.

The locks built on the St. Lawrence during this period are almost identical in size to those that had been designed for the Welland Canal in the early twentieth century. Five of the locks are located on the Canadian side of the St. Lawr-

ence and two on the United States side. The minimum depth of the new section was 8.2 metres (27 feet) and the rest of the system, including the Welland Canal and the connecting channels, was brought to this standard. Thus, by the early 1960s, the depth of 8.2 metres (27 feet) was available over the entire route from Montreal to Lake Superior. The St. Lawrence Seaway had come into existence.

Enquiries for information should be directed to: Information Officer, St. Lawrence Seaway Authority, Transport Canada, Tower A, Place de Ville, Ottawa, Ontario. U.S. Agency: St. Lawrence Seaway Development Corporation, Box 520, Seaway Circle, Massena, N.Y.

Publications, free, text in English and French, include:

• **Brochure: The St. Lawrence Seaway.** Summary data about the history of the Seaway and its present characteristics, including diagrams of the system.

- **Fact Sheet: The Montreal - Lake Ontario Section of the Seaway.** Outlines history, Canada - U.S. negotiations, construction, locks, ships and traffic.

- **Fact Sheet: The Welland Section of the Seaway.** Outlines history of each Canal, the present locks, improvements, lock procedures, and the Canal as a trade artery.

- Annual publications include **The Seaway: Operations, Outlook, Statistics** and **Annual Report.**

The Seaway Handbook contains regulations for use of the Seaway (including the Welland Canal) by vessels. The 1980 consolidated edition replaces previous issues of the St. Lawrence Seaway **Master's Handbook** and **Seaway Handbook.**

4.2 A Marine Career

A constant demand exists for highly skilled masters, mates and crews. Expansion of the Canadian foreign and inland fleet will continue to provide excellent career opportunities for Canadian men and women. Other developments will also increase the demand. One is the rotation system of crews which will allow a ship to remain operational for extended periods.

There are two ways to become a Canadian merchant service sailor. One is to become a navigation or engineering officer. The other is to work your way up the ladder through shipboard experience. Grade 12 graduation is sufficient for entry into officer training or cadet programs operated by various colleges throughout Canada. Typically, a year consists of six months of at-sea training and six months of classroom studies. The courses usually last three years and, on graduation, you can become either a navigation or an engineering officer.

The average annual income for officers in their first year aboard ships belonging to the Dominion Marine Association after graduation is $23,000.00. By accumulating sea experience and passing further exams, officers can qualify for positions of higher responsibility and pay. For further information, contact the Canadian Marine Officer's Union, 2 Albert Street West, Thorold.

The other way to go to sea is to sign on a vessel as a deckhand. To do this you apply to the respective union and sign up at the hiring hall. The unions involved are the Seafarers International Union of Canada (70 St. David's Street East, Thorold, or 634 St. James Street West, Montreal) and the Canadian Brotherhood of Railway, Transport and General Workers (2300 Carling Avenue, Ottawa). By accumulating sea-time and additional shipboard skills, you can qualify for a higher rating. For more detailed information regarding a career in the merchant service, contact the nearest college or union.

Colleges offering officer training programs:

Georgian College of Applied Arts & Technology, Owen Sound Campus, 1150 8th St. E., Owen Sound, Ontario.

Niagara College of Applied Arts & Technology, Woodlawn Road, Welland, Ontario.

Quebec Maritime Institute, 167 rue St.-Louis, Rimouski, Quebec.

St. Lawrence College, Cornwall Campus, Windmill Point, Cornwall, Ontario.

College of Fisheries, St. John's, P.O. Box 4920, Newfoundland.

4.3 The Welland Canal Mission

The Welland Canal Mission has provided continuous service since 1868 to the men and women aboard ships traversing the Welland Canal. Only four men have served as Chaplain. Thomas Bone visited old sailing schooners and wooden steamers until 1906; James Judson, his successor, saw steam fully replace sail. Cameron Orr took over the work in 1939, and witnessed the effects of opening the St. Lawrence Seaway. The current Chaplain, Arthur Taylor, has been calling aboard ships since 1972.

The Chaplain provides spiritual counsel to those who, by the very nature of their job, cannot attend regular services. An ability to listen has always been a vital ingredient, but more practical work includes hospital and home visits, weddings and funerals. An interdenominational ministry, the Chaplain offers a prayer of dedication when ships are christened, and he speaks at churches throughout Ontario to describe the work. For more information contact the Chaplain at 81 Dorothy Street, St. Catharines.

4.4 Canal Data

Movable Bridges:

Number	Location	Type	Traffic
1	Lock 1, Lakeshore Road, St. Catharines	Rolling Lift (single)	Highway/rail/1 sidewalk
3A	Lock 2, Carlton St., St. Catharines	Rolling Lift (single)	Highway/1 sidewalk
4	Regional Road 81, Queenston St., St. Catharines	Rolling Lift (double)	Highway/2 sidewalks
5	Glendale Avenue, St. Catharines	Vertical Lift	Highway/2 sidewalks
6	Lock 4, CN, St. Catharines	Rolling Lift (2 spans, single)	Rail
10	CN, Thorold	Vertical Lift	Rail
11	Highway 20, Allanburg	Vertical Lift	Highway/2 sidewalks
19	Lock 8 (north), Highway 3, Main St., Port Colborne	Rolling Lift (single)	Highway/2 sidewalks
20	CN, Port Colborne	Vertical Lift	Rail
21	Clarence Street, Port Colborne	Vertical Lift	Highway/2 sidewalks

Locks:

Locks	Location	Normal Lift m.	Usable Length m.	Width of Chamber m.
Lock 1	Lakeshore Road, St. Catharines	14.02 (46.0')	222.50 (730')	24.38 (80')
Lock 2	Carlton Street, St. Catharines	14.17 (46.5')	222.50 (730')	24.38 (80')
Lock 3	Government Road, St. Catharines	14.17 (46.5')	222.50 (730')	24.38 (80')
Lock 4	Government Road, St. Catharines	14.60 (47.9')	222.50 (730')	24.38 (80')
Lock 5	Canal Road, Thorold	14.60 (47.9')	222.50 (730')	24.38 (80')
Lock 6	Canal Road, Thorold	13.32 (43.7')	222.50 (730')	24.38 (80')
Lock 7	Canal Road, Thorold	14.17 (46.5')	222.50 (730')	24.38 (80')
Lock 8	Highway 3 (Main St.), Port Colborne	0.61-3.35 (2'-11')	349.91 (1148')	24.38 (80')

Traffic on the Welland Canal, 1980

Selected Commodities		Tonnes	Percent	Change over 1979 Percentages
Agricultural Products:				
Wheat		14,294,910	24.0	-35.6
Corn		6,773,349	11.4	-9.2
Rye		502,926	.8	+147.8
Oats		314,490	.5	+102.5
Barley		2,266,327	3.8	-33.5
Soybeans		1,667,976	2.8	-2.7
Flaxseed		252,852	.4	-22.5
Other Grains		2,076,325	3.5	-10.6
Total Grains		28,149,155	47.2	+7.7
Other Agricultural Products		107,785	.2	-27.7
	TOTAL	28,256,940	47.4	+7.5
Mine Products:				
Iron Ore		11,417,850	19.2	-24.5
Coal		7,292,903	12.2	-6.4
Coke		1,434,884	2.4	-42.7
Stone, Ground, Crushed, or Rough		1,155,014	1.9	-24.5
Salt		1,417,627	2.4	-5.0
Other Mine Products		1,299,321	2.2	-11.2
	TOTAL	24,017,599	40.3	-19.7
Processed Products:				
Iron and Steel		1,318,704	2.2	-54.6
Fuel Oil		1,664,553	2.8	-0.6
Other Petroleum Products		357,827	.6	-12.1
Chemicals		625,678	1.0	+1.5
Other Processed Products		2,908,671	4.9	-26.2
	TOTAL	6,875,433	11.5	-28.0
Miscellaneous Cargo:				
Forest Products		35,636	-	-46.1
Animal Products		153,243	.3	+18.2
Package Freight		267 130	.5	+6.8
	TOTAL	456,009	.3	+2.3
	GRAND TOTAL	59,605,981	100.00	-9.9

Total Length . . 23.45 nautical miles (27.0 miles)
Total Lift . . . . 100 m (327 feet)
Width of bottom: generally . . . 59 m (192 feet)
      :Welland By-Pass . . . . . . 107 m (350 feet)
Width of water surface
      :generally . . . . 94 m (310 feet)
      :Welland By-Pass . . . . . . 152 m (500 feet)
Depth of Canal prism
      :generally . . . . 8.2 m (27 feet)
Minimum overhead clearance:
      lift and fixed bridges . . . 36.6 m (120 feet)
Minimum overhead clearance: power
      and telephone lines . . . . 39.6 m (130 feet)
Maximum vessel dimensions:
      Overall length . . . . . . 222.5 m (730 feet)
      Extreme breadth . . . . . . 23.16 m (76 feet)
      Maximum height above
        water level . . . . 35.5 m (116.5 feet)
      Draught   79.25 dm or decimetres (26 feet)
Minimum vessel dimensions:
      No vessel of less than 6.10 m (20 feet) in
      overall length, or 907.18 kg (1 ton) in
      weight, shall transit
Maximum vessel speeds:
      7.7 knots (9 mph) through the Welland By-
      Pass; elsewhere, 6.1 knots (7 mph)

Some Comparative Statistics:

A Comparison Between the Welland, Suez and Panama Canals

The Welland Canal is the older waterway, though the Suez and the Panama are older as Ship Canals. The Suez, opened to navigation in 1869, linked the Mediterranean to the Red Sea, which made it the shortest navigable route between the East and the West and avoided the circuitous route via the Cape of Good Hope. The Suez, the longest canal in the world with no locks, now allows the transit of vessels up to 150,000 tonnes fully loaded; they transit the Canal in three convoys daily, two southbound and one northbound. The Suez has been closed five times, most seriously for eight years after the 1967 War.

The Panama Canal was opened to navigation in 1914 to link the Atlantic to the Pacific ocean. It is a lock-type canal, approximately 82 kilometres (51 miles) long. Vessels transiting the Canal are raised in three steps to the level of Gatun Lake, the principal source of canal water, then lowered to sea level again in three steps. The three set of canal locks are paired, which permits simultaneous lockages of two vessels.

	Welland Canal	Suez Canal	Panama Canal
Opening Date: First Canal	1829		
Fourth Canal	1932	1869	1914
Length (km)	42	179	82
Width (m)	58.4/107.7	170	152
Maximum Draught (m)	7.92 (26 feet)	16.68 (53 feet)	11.89 (39 feet)
Locks	8	no	6 (twin)
Maximum deadweight of Transit Vessel	30,000	150,000	n/a
Tonnage, 1979 (Million Tonnes)	66.2	163.2	157.0
Number of Transits, 1979	6,547	20,363	14,363
Operational Period	April 1 - December 31	12 months	12 months
Flags	30	104	70
Toll Revenues (Canadian $ in millions)	21.3	588.0	209.5

4.5 A Chronological Outline of Canal Evolution

1818 Survey from the head waters of the Twelve Mile Creek to the Chippawa Creek (Welland River) by William Hamilton Merritt, and others.

The First Welland Canal, 1829-1844

1824 The Welland Canal Company was incorporated as a private company, and the first sod to initiate the Canal works was turned at Allanburg.

1825 New plans were adopted. Entrance agreed at Port Dalhousie from Lake Ontario.

1829 Two schooners were passed through the completed Canal to Buffalo. Boats could be towed between Lake Erie and Lake Ontario in about one day.

1833 Work started in 1831 to carry the Canal from Port Robinson to Lake Erie at Port Colborne. A direct Lake-to-Lake communication by canal had been achieved for the first time.

The Second Welland Canal, 1845-1915

1841 The Government of Upper Canada purchased the entire Canal from its private stockholders.

1842 Work started on the project for deepening the Canal, the conversion of the Feeder Canal into a navigable canal, the construction of a branch from the Feeder to Port Maitland, and the replacement of the wooden locks with durable stone structures.

1845 The Canal, with 27 stone locks and a nine-foot (2.74 m) depth of water on the sills, was completed from Port Dalhousie to Welland. The Feeder branch to Dunnville, as well as the Port Maitland branch, were also completed to Canal standards.

1853 The Welland Railway was under construction between Port Dalhousie and Port Colborne, so that ships could be made lighter for the canal passage.

1854 The Reciprocity Treaty with the United States permitted its shipping to use the Canal.

1855 The navigable depth of the Canal was increased between 1853 and 1855 to ten feet, by raising the banks and the walls of the locks and by dredging.

1881 The work, inaugurated in 1846 to lower the summit level of the Canal, was achieved by 1881. Since this date, the Canal has been supplied with water direct from Lake Erie at Port Colborne.

1887 The Third Canal was opened along a new route from Port Dalhousie to Allanburg, but the Second Canal between Port Dalhousie and Thorold remained in operation for navigation until 1915.

The Third Welland Canal, 1887-1930

1871 The Dominion Government took control of the Canal at Confederation, and a Commission recommended a uniform scale of navigation for the St. Lawrence route and the Welland Canal with 12 feet (3.66 m) of water over the sills.

1873 Work started on construction to a 12-foot (8.66 m) depth, increased to 14 feet (4.27 m) in 1875.

1887 The Canal was opened for navigation with a 14-foot (4.27 m) depth. The route from Port Dalhousie lay east of the Second Canal, diagonally across the present city of St. Catharines, and along a more direct route between Thorold and Allanburg. The route of the Second Canal was then enlarged and deepened to Port Colborne. There were 25 stone lift locks, one guard lock, an aqueduct at Welland to carry the Canal over the Welland River, and harbour improvements at Port Colborne and Port Dalhousie.

1901 The St. Lawrence Canals were opened with a 14-foot (4.27 m) navigational channel. About 620,000 tonnes passed through the Third Canal in 1901, 3.9 million tonnes in 1914, and 7.4 million tonnes in 1928.

1930 The last year in which the Third Canal system was in commission, but the entrance lock at Port Dalhousie continued to function until 1969. The Third Canal, between Ramey's Bend and Port Colborne, also remained in use as a raceway to supply the Fourth Canal and the hydro-electric establishment at Decew with water.

The Fourth Welland Canal, 1931-Present

1895 A Deep Waterway Commission reported on possible waterways connecting the Great Lakes and the Atlantic Ocean. The first works of construction at a larger scale,

completed by 1908, included a government grain elevator and large breakwaters at Port Colborne, and the deepening of this harbour to 22 feet (6.7 m). The elevator was increased in capacity in 1912-1913, and again in 1923-1924.

1913 The Ten Mile Creek route was adopted for the northern stretch of the Fourth Canal, and the requisite engineering works were initiated. A new artificial harbour was created at Port Weller. The Canal then followed the former valley of Ten Mile Creek to the foot of the Escarpment at Thorold, where the slope was climbed abruptly by four locks. The Channel then followed a more direct line to the inner harbour of Port Colborne.

1931 Vessels of St. Lawrence Canal size with a draft of 18 feet (5.49 m) were allowed through the Welland Canal, increased to 22 feet (6.7 m) in 1932. By 1934, *"the Canal between Port Weller and Port Robinson is generally excavated to a minimum depth of 25 feet [7.62 m] and between Port Robinson and Port Colborne to 27-1/2 feet [8.38 m], and the harbours of Port Weller and Port Colborne to 28 feet [8.53 m] below standard low water level of the lakes. All the structures of the canal have, however, been built for an ultimate depth of 30 feet [9.14 m] which can be obtained at any time in the future, should the demands of navigation require it, by the simple process of dredging the canal reaches and harbours without interfering with navigation. Only 20 feet [6.1 m] is at present available at low water level in the harbours and channels of the Upper Lakes".*

1951 The St. Lawrence Seaway Authority was constituted for the purpose of constructing, maintaining and operating a deep waterway between the Port of Montreal and the Upper Great Lakes. The first contracts were awarded in 1954, when construction work began.

1959 The Seaway locks on the St. Lawrence River were opened. Dredging had been undertaken to bring the channels of the Fourth Canal up to the Seaway standards of 25.5 feet (7.77 m) for the draught of vessels. The Department of Transport also turned the Welland Canal over to the St. Lawrence Seaway Authority at this date, and it has since been operated and maintained as an integral part of the Seaway.

1966 Proposals were announced for the enlargement of the system, including a new channel to replace the winding and narrow channel passing through the City of Welland, a new alignment to the east of the present Fourth Canal along its northern stretch past St. Catharines, and the replacement of all lift locks at the Escarpment with locks of larger lift and dimensions. Four locks with an average lift of more than 80 feet (26.25 m) were envisaged.

1967 A progressive lockage charge was introduced, rising to $800 for a complete passage by 1971.

1968 The Thorold Tunnel was opened, and Bridges 7 and 9 closed and dismantled to provide for the freer movements for vessels.

1973 The Welland Canal By-Pass was opened. Extending from Port Robinson to Ramey's Bend across the southern or higher extent of the Niagara Peninsula, it retired from active service the former winding channel through the commercial heart of Welland. The new channel is 8.3 miles (13.35 km) long, compared with a 9.1 mile (14.64 km) length for its predecessor. It is also straighter, wider, deeper and offers no obstruction to navigation along its length.

1979 150th Anniversary of opening the First Welland Canal.

4.6 Regional Travel and Tourist Information

The Region Niagara Tourist Council encourages and promotes tourism in the municipalities that comprise the Regional Municipality of Niagara. It operates tourist information centres, collects and disseminates brochures, distributes press releases and newsletters, assists in organizing conventions and conferences, answers mail and telephone inquiries, produces and distributes tourist brochures including one on the Welland Canal. For this brochure, or for information on tourist attractions in the Region, contact the Region Niagara Tourist Council, 227 Church Street, P.O. Box 3025, St. Catharines, Ontario.

For information about the Canal and its tourist facilities contact:
• Chamber of Commerce, 76 Main Street, West, Port Colborne.
• Chamber of Commerce, 132 King Street, St. Catharines.
• Chamber of Commerce, 55 Main Street, East, Welland.
Seasonal locations along the Canal include:
• Lock 3, Tourist Information Booth, Canal Road, St. Catharines.
• Lock 8, Tourist Information Centre, Port Colborne near Bridge 19.
• Ontario Government Travel Information, Garden City Skyway, St. Catharines.

4.7 Regional Canal Associations

Rehabilitate the Old Feeder Canal Association

This organization is an active and concerned lobby for the Welland Feeder Canal, the abandoned remains of which lie within the municipalities of Welland, Wainfleet and Dunnville. Its construction in 1829 made possible the First Welland Canal, and nurtured communities along its length. The Association prepared *A Feasibility Study on the Welland Feeder Canal* in 1979. Enquiries to Rehabilitate the Old Feeder Canal Association, Box 54, Wainfleet, Ontario.

The Welland Canals Foundation

The Welland Canals Foundation is successor to Welland Canal 150th Anniversary Inc., formed in 1979 to bring the historic significance of the Welland Canals into prominence upon the sesquicentennial of the completion of the First Welland Canal in 1829. The continuing organization co-ordinates the activities of various groups dealing with aspects of the four Canals. The Foundation also seeks to generate publicity and promotion, publications, and to co-ordinate special events such as a series of *"Canal Days"* planned for the summer months. Enquiries to The Secretary, Welland Canals Foundation, P.O. Box 745, St. Catharines.

The Welland Canals Preservation Association

The Welland Canals Preservation Association was founded as a non-profit corporation to preserve, restore and develop a recreational corridor along the routes of the old Welland Canals. The construction of a rustic bicycle/hiking trail through the Canal valley of St. Catharines, and Mountain Locks Park at Mountain Street and Glendale Avenue in St. Catharines, were the first projects. Eventual plans are for the park system to be extended along former Canal routes from Port Dalhousie to Port Colborne. The Association is supported by local businesses, industries, and the municipal, provincial and federal levels of government. Annual membership $5.00. Enquiries to Welland Canals Preservation Association, 52 Lakeport Road, P.O. Box 1224, St. Catharines.

A Canadian Canals Society was initiated in May 1982. Enquiries to the Secretary, Dr. R.R. Taylor, Department of History, Brock University, St. Catharines, Ontario.

4.8 Regional Libraries

Brock University

The Main Library is housed in the Tower, DeCew Campus, St. Catharines. The collection of books, periodicals, microfilms, newspapers and government documents covers many aspects of both the present and former Canal systems, and the associated evolution of settlement, industry and landscape in the Niagara Peninsula. This regional collection is one area of emphasis for the Brock Library with many of the rarer and more expensive books and materials published in, or dealing with, the Niagara Peninsula being housed in the Special Collections room on Floor 2. Author, subject and title indexes are available in the Main Collection and in Government Documents. There is access by the national Telex networks of libraries for the quick location of material not available in the Library. Guides to services provided through the Library are available.

The Map Library is located in Room C207 of the East Block in the Department of Geography. The collection includes many items concerned with the Welland Canals and the Niagara Peninsula: photographic and xerographic copies of maps in Federal and Provincial Archives, engineering plans of the Fourth Canal, topographic maps from 1904 onwards, nautical charts, aerial photographs from 1921 to the present, and exhibit collections of maps, photographs and airphoto mosaics.

Port Colborne Public Library

The Port Colborne Public Library on King Street in downtown Port Colborne has books and pamphlets on the Welland Canal in its Local History Collection. These include histories, studies, proceedings and tourist guides. The Local History Vertical Files contain some additional pamphlets, pictures and photographs, typescripts of local research papers, and newspaper clippings from 1957 to the present. A taped interview (uncatalogued) with Erie Carter, daughter of the late Dewitt Carter (President of the Welland Canal Tug Company and Canal historian) includes some original information on the Canal. A typed transcript of this tape is available.

St. Catharines Centennial Public Library

St. Catharines Centennial Public Library at 54 Church Street, in downtown St. Catharines, houses the Special Collections Room which contains a resource centre for information on the Welland Canals. Included are books on the history and development of the Canals, the impact of the Canals on community development, and related studies regarding present and future plans. The Room has copies of most theses written about the Canal. Microfilm holdings include the Merritt Papers and early Niagara Peninsula newspapers. There are also extensive newspaper clipping files on related subjects.

Welland Public Library

The Welland Public Library at 140 King Street in downtown Welland has prepared a Selective Bibliography of material available for use through the Local History section in the Reference Department of the Library. The collection is not exhaustive, but it consists of many important books, pamphlets, maps, newspaper articles, photographs and micro-material which underline the historical, social and economic development of Welland and the Welland Canal in its vicinity.

4.9 Regional Museums

Port Colborne Historical and Marine Museum

The Port Colborne Historical and Marine Museum at 280 King Street in downtown Port Colborne, one block west of the Canal, houses exhibits on the history of all four Canals. It includes ship models, navigational aids and equipment. On the grounds is the wheelhouse of a tug, outfitted and ready for young sailors to take over; a marine receiver enables visitors to listen to the Seaway Traffic Control in St. Catharines guiding ships in and out of the locks at Port Colborne. The Museum has pictures and maps of the Canal and Port Colborne's vicinity from 1866 to the present, books covering related areas of history, a list of shipwrecks on the Great Lakes 1870 to 1979, and an excellent post card collection.

St. Catharines Historical Museum

St. Catharines Historical Museum at 343 Merritt Street in Merritton explains the significance of the four Canals in the growth of St. Catharines in two galleries. Displays include a model lock, a diving suit, a finely detailed ship's model, and photographs illustrating Canal history. The Museum houses an extensive collection of books, reports, and histories dealing with the Canals; microfilm holdings and archival material relating to shipping company records, vessels register and insurance classifications, Canal business records, shipping company records, and the personal papers of W.H. Merritt; and maps, plans, diagrams, photographs, engravings and post cards of the Canals.

Welland Historical Museum

The Welland Historical Museum at 660 South Pelham Street between Welland and Fonthill houses a collection of articles pertaining to the development and growth of Welland, its industries and its series of Canals. The collection includes several mounted and unmounted photographs, together with reference sources and other materials in the archives.

4.10 Audio-Visual Material

Double Image Packages

Drs. Roberta M. Styran and Robert R. Taylor, Department of History, Brock University, have produced two units which use taped dialogue synchronized with two slide projectors. Users, providing their own carousel, projectors and screens, may borrow free of charge the two drums of slides, the stereo tape, and the playback machine from either the Instructional Media Centre, Brock University, St. Catharines, or the Welland Canals Preservation Association, P.O. Box 1224, St. Catharines.

- *St. Catharines: A City the Canals Built*

13 minutes long, 160 colour slides. The many ways in which the four Welland Canals have helped to build St. Catharines are discussed: sources of power for factories; jobs and prosperity in general; and recreation. How have the streets and buildings of the City been influenced by the Canals?

- *Niagara's Neglected Treasures*

20 minutes long; 151 colour slides. The ruinous condition of the abandoned locks and waterways of the First, Second and Third Canals is compared to the conservation practices in other communities with historic canal facilities. The potential of Niagara's Canal lands as recreational areas, historic sites, and tourist attractions is examined. Suggestions for the future are offered.

Films

Farr Films, 14 Swallow Crescent, Hamilton.

- *The Welland Canal ... Merritt's Folly*

16 mm film, 23 minutes long, in colour: An overview of the Canal based on an interview with actor David MacKenzie as William Hamilton Merritt. Many still photographs and sketches are used, as well as maps and diagrams. A teacher's guide and workbook are available.

Geovisuals, Box 869, Waterloo, Ontario. Catalogue No. 17. Price $25.80 per set, including notes:

30 slides for use in the geography classroom, providing historic detail on Canals 1, 2 and 3; present Canal, locks 1 to 8, operations, bridges and tunnels.

The National Film Board of Canada, Box 6100, Montreal, Quebec:

- *Story of the St. Lawrence Seaway*

16 mm film, 12:53 minutes long, in colour, catalogue number 106C 0159 008: Describes Seaway project from conception to completion, from the early fur trade to June 1959. Animated drawings show the profile of the waterway.

- *Seaway to the Heartland*

16 mm film, 27:37 minutes long, in colour, catalogue number 106C 0175 700: The story of the St. Lawrence Seaway, its construction, its operation and its impact on our economy, including a brief historical review of the earlier canals which were built as long as 200 years ago.

The Ontario Educational Communications Authority, Box 200, Station Q, Toronto:

- *The Greatest Inland Waterway in the World*

On videotape to non-profit educational institutions in Ontario, or on view in screening rooms in Toronto by advance appointment, 29 minutes long, in colour, series title Behind the Shield, 184204. Hosts Scott Symons and Mary Kay Ross discuss Ontarians' reluctance to recognize their entrepreneurial heroes, and consider the remarkable achievements of William Hamilton Merritt, who proposed and built the first Welland Canal in the 1820s. Merritt, played by actor David MacKenzie, talks with Ross about his original vision for the great inland waterway.

Kit for Elementary Schools

Available from the Instructional Resource Centre, College of Education, Brock University, St. Catharines.

- K1022 includes, *inter alia,* a slide set on The Welland Canal in Thorold's History; document portfolios on Lewis Shickluna, shipping business in the Niagara Peninsula and William Hamilton Merritt; and a Welland Canal Game.

4.11 General Interest Courses

In addition to its Degree credit courses, Brock University offers general interest courses which normally include aspects of life in the Niagara Peninsula, including Canal related themes. These courses are open to everyone; they require neither previous experience nor prerequisites, and they do not lead to certificates, diplomas or degrees. Instead, they present an opportunity for organized reading and writing, and to exchange ideas with instructors and fellow students. Details from the Part Time Programs Office, Brock University, St. Catharines.

The Brock University Speakers' Bureau provides speakers for schools, clubs, community groups and association meetings. Topics include the Peninsula and the Canal. Details from the Liaison and Information Officer, Brock University, St. Catharines.

From time to time Niagara College of Applied Arts and Technology offers general interest courses on themes related to the Welland Canal. These courses examine the historical development and impact of the Canal on various communities, and on-site programs such as *"Let's Explore the Canal"* give students a chance to view the working aspects of the Canal such as its bridges, locks and ships. An annual CANAL CRUISE, a one-day excursion through the entire Canal aboard a small passenger ship, is always most successful. Details from Continuing Education Services, Niagara College of Applied Arts and Technology, Box 1005, Welland.

4.12 Canal Societies

People interested in ships may wish to join one of the Canal Societies. There are plenty to choose from and they meet a wide range of interest. Some are associated with museums and most have regular publications.

• American Canal Society, quarterly *American Canals.* Contact Charles W. Derr, Secretary-Treasurer, 117 Main Street, Freemansburg, Pa. 18017. Membership, $8.00 U.S.

• Great Lakes Historical Society, quarterly *Inland Seas.* Contact Great Lakes Historical Society, 480 Main Street, Vermilion, Ohio 44089. Membership, $12.00.

• Great Lakes Maritime Institute, bi-monthly *Telescope.* Contact Great Lakes Maritime Institute, Dossin Museum, 100 The Strand, Belle Isle, Detroit, Michigan 48207. Membership, $7.00 U.S., $8.50 Canadian.

• Marine Historical Society of Detroit, monthly *Detroit Marine Historian.* Contact Mr. Bill Luke, Marine Historical Society of Detroit, 20255 Wellesley Blvd., Birmingham, Michigan 48010. Membership, $8.00 U.S.

• Steamship Historical Society of America, quarterly *Steamship Bill,* deals with passenger fleets past and present. Contact Mrs. Susan Ewen, Steamship Historical Society of America, 170 Westminster Street, Room 1103, Providence, Rhode Island 02903. Membership, $15.00 U.S.

• Toronto Marine Historical Society, 9 issues per year of *Scanner.* Contact Mr. Jim Kidd, Toronto Marine Historical Society, 83 Humberview Road, Toronto, Ontario. Membership, $10.00.

4.13 Bibliography

Aitken, Hugh G.J. *The Welland Canal Company: A Study In Canadian Enterprise.* Cambridge, Mass., Harvard University Press, 1954. 178 p. illus.
>An investigation of the role of the Welland Canal Company in the building of the First Welland Canal.

Canada. Dept. of Railways and Canals. *The Opening Of The Welland Ship Canal, August sixth, nineteen thirty-two.* Ottawa, King's Printer, 1932. 43 p. illus.
>A descriptive account of the construction of the Fourth Canal, issued for the official opening.

Cowan, P.J. *The Welland Ship Canal Between Lake Ontario And Lake Erie, 1913-1932.* London, Offices of *"Engineering"*, 1935. 254 p. illus.
>Reprint of articles describing the construction of the Fourth Canal which appeared in *"Engineering"* during 1929-1931.

Creighton, Ogden. *General View Of The Welland Canal, In The Province of Upper Canada: Together With A Brief Examination Of Its Advantages.* London, England, Printed for J. Miller, 1830. 23 p.
>A summary of the benefits of the new Canal, opened in 1829.

Gillham, E.B. (Skip). *The Best Of Ships Along The Seaway.* St. Catharines, Stonehouse Publications, 1981. 60 p. illus.

Gillham, E.B. (Skip). *Ships Along The Seaway.* Fonthill, Stonehouse Publications, 1971-1975, 2 v. (52, 60 p.) illus.
>Documentary details about ships that use the Welland Canal.

Gillham, E.B. (Skip). *The Welland Canal Mission.* St. Catharines, printed for the Welland Canal Mission to Sailors by Stonehouse Publications, 1981. 40 p. illus.
>A history of the Welland Canal Mission to Sailors.

Greenwald, Michelle. *The Welland Canals: Historical Resource Analysis And Preservation Alternatives.* By Michelle Greenwald, Alan Levitt and Elaine Peebles. Rev. ed. Toronto, Ontario Ministry of Culture and Recreation, 1977. 175 p. illus. And *The Welland Canals Study: A Summary.* Toronto, 1976. 11 p.
>A study of the heritage potential of the former Welland Canals.

Greenwood, John O. and Dills, Michael J. *Greenwood's And Dill's Lake Boats '81.* Cleveland, Ohio, Freshwater Press, 1981. illus.
>A comprehensive account of lake shipping, published annually.

Heisler, John P. *The Canals of Canada.* (Canadian Historic Sites: Occasional Papers In Archaeology And History, no. 8). Ottawa, Dept. of Indian Affairs and Northern Development, 1973. 183 p. illus.

A detailed account of the historical development of the Canadian canal system.

Illustrated Historical Atlas Of The Counties Of Lincoln And Welland. Compiled by H.R. Page. Toronto, A. Craig Steam Litho., 1876. Reprinted by R. Cumming, Port Elgin, Ont., 1971. 83 p. illus.

Jackson, John N. *St. Catharines, Ontario: Its Early Years.* Belleville, Mika, 1976. 416 p. illus.

A history of St. Catharines, showing the influence of the Canals on the growth of the City and regional settlement along the Canal to the 1860s.

Jackson, John N. *Welland And The Welland Canal: The Welland Canal By-Pass.* Belleville, Mika, 1975. 214 p. illus.

A decription of the construction and effects of the Welland Canal By-Pass around the City of Welland.

Kemp, Peter, ed. *The Oxford Companion To Ships And The Sea,* London, Eng., Oxford University Press, 1976. 972 p. illus.

An encyclopedia about ships.

Legget, Robert F. *Canals Of Canada.* Vancouver, Douglas, David and Charles, 1976. 261 p. illus.

A discussion of the role and significance of the Canadian canal system.

Legget, Robert F. *The Seaway.* Toronto, Clarke Irwin, 1979. 92 p. illus.

An official publication to mark the 20th anniversary of the Seaway and the 150th anniversary of the First Welland Canal.

Linden, Rev. Peter J. Van der, ed. *Great Lakes Ships We Remember.* Cleveland, Ohio, Freshwater Press, 1979. 413 p. illus.

Ships and the shipping industry on the Great Lakes.

Macht, Wally. *The First 50 Years: A History Of Upper Lakes Shipping, Ltd.* Toronto, Virgo Press, 1981. 120 p. illus.

An account of the ships in the fleet of this company.

Martine, Gloria. *The Role Of The Welland Canal In Industrial Location.* Toronto, Dept. of Geography, University of Toronto, 1961. 61 leaves (B.A. thesis).

Examines the influence of the Canal upon industries in the Niagara Peninsula.

Meaney, Carl Frank Patrick. *The Welland Canal And Canadian Development.* Hamilton, McMaster University, 1980. 126 leaves (draft of M.A. thesis).

An examination of the men associated in the construction and development of the First Canal.

Merritt, William Hamilton. **Biography Of The Hon. W.H. Meritt, M.P.** Compiled principally from his original diary and correspondence, by J.P. Merritt. St. Catharines, E.S. Leavenworth, 1875. 429 p.

A biography by Merritt's son, based on excerpts from Merritt's own diary and correspondence.

Merritt, William Hamilton. **Brief Review Of The Origin, Progress, Present State And Future Prospects Of The Welland Canal.** St. Catharines, H. Leavenworth, 1853. 48 p.

Reviews the past and future potential of the Welland Canal.

Mitchener, David M. **The Canals At Welland.** Welland, Rotary Club of Welland, 1973. 46 p. illus.

A description of the Canals in the City of Welland.

Misener, Ralph S. **The Great Lakes/Seaway: Setting A Course For The '80s. A Report Of The Provincial Great Lakes/Seaway Task Force.** Toronto, Task Force, 1981. 88 p. illus.

An assessment by the Chairman of the Task Force of present character and future needs, recommending new facilities.

Petrie, Francis J. **Canal Development In The Niagara Peninsula.** Ottawa, St. Lawrence Seaway Authority, 1967. 16 p.

Printed programme issued to mark the beginning of the Welland Channel relocation, June 9, 1967.

Pritchard, Jean. **The Welland Canal, Yesterday, Today, Tomorrow.** Rev. ed. Written and compiled by Jean Pritchard; art work and maps by Alain Pritchard; edited by Francis J. Petrie. Port Robinson, Jean Pritchard Publications, 1975. 28 p. illus.

A brief account of the former and present Canals.

Rehabilitate the Old Feeder Canal Association, Inc. **A Feasibility Study On The Welland Feeder Canal.** Wainfleet, 1979. 206 leaves. illus.

A report on the historical importance and recreational potential of the Old Feeder Canal.

Runnalls, J. Lawrence. **The Irish On The Welland Canal.** St. Catharines, St. Catharines Public Library, 1973. 65 p. illus.

An examination of the role of the Irish in the construction of the Welland Canal.

Taylor, Robert Stanley. **The Historical Development Of The Four Welland Canals, 1824-1933.** London, University of Western Ontario, 1950. 228 leaves. illus. (M.A. thesis).

An examination of the development of the four Welland Canals.

Upper Canada, House of Assembly. Select Committee Appointed To Examine And Enquire Into The Management Of The Welland Canal. **Third Report From The Select Committee...** Toronto, William Lyon Mackenzie, Office of the Constitution, 1836. 575 p.

An exhaustive examination into the management of the Welland Canal Company.

Welland Canal Company. ***The Annual Report Of The Board Of Directors Of The Welland Canal Company.*** St. Catharines, H. Leavenworth, 1825-1832.

Primary historical material about the First Welland Canal.

Welland Canal Company. ***Letter Book 1823-1876,*** 7 volumes. Microfilm, 2 reels.

Correspondence revealing the organization and management of the first three Canals.

Welland Canal Company. ***Minutes Of The Welland Canal Company,*** 1825-1837. Microfilm, 1 reel.

The decisions and actions of the private Welland Canal Company.

The Welland Canals: Proceedings Of The First Annual Niagara Peninsula History Conference, April 21-22, 1979. Edited by John Burtniak and Wesley B. Turner. St. Catharines, Brock University. 1979. 85 p. illus.

A collection of papers dealing with various aspects of the Welland Canals delivered at the Conference marking the 150th anniversary of the opening of the First Welland Canal.